"In this remarkably readable b[...] of Jesus reported in the Bible and throughout history. Included is a discussion of the image of Jesus on the Shroud of Turin and his own careful study of thirty contemporary encounters with Jesus. Phillip Wiebe makes the strongest possible case that while maybe only limited experimental evidence from which decisions about encounters with Jesus can be made, the experiential evidence is more than persuasive and is foundational for the faith commitments of many."

—**Ralph W. Hood Jr.,** PhD, professor, former president of the Division of Psychology of Religion of the American Psychological Association, recipient of its William James Award, and author of *The Psychology of Religion*, 4th ed. (with Peter Hill and Bernard Spilka) and *Them that Believe* (with W. Paul Williamson)

"Phillip Wiebe's *Visions and Appearances of Jesus* makes available to the non-specialist reader the results of his extensive investigation and analysis of claimed perceptual appearances of Jesus. In light of Wiebe's careful and judicious approach, always avoiding the temptation to claim more than the evidence warrants, his conclusion that naturalistic explanations of such experiences fail badly is hard to dispute. This is a book that deserves to be read by both sceptic and Christian alike."

—**Robert Larmer,** PhD, professor and chair of the department of philosophy, University of New Brunswick, author of *Water Into Wine? An Investigation of the Concept of Miracle* (McGill-Queen's University Press, 1988), "The Meaning of Miracles" in *The Cambridge Companion to Miracles*, ed. Graham H. Twelftree (Cambridge University Press, 2011), *The Legitimacy of Miracle* (Lexington, Press, 2014)

"Jesus' apostles believed that the time between his first and second coming would be one during which his followers would dream dreams and see visions. Philip Wiebe's new book gathers just some of the vast testimonial 'evidence' for such phenomena, not only reaching back through Christian history but also documenting and preserving a range of interesting present-day accounts. Such a non-sensationalistic, informed, and yet eminently accessible treatment is incalculably valuable as it invites thoughtful people, believers and skeptics alike, to reconsider matters of faith and reason that oftentimes are dismissed prematurely."

—**Amos Yong,** author of *Who is the Holy Spirit: A Walk with the Apostles*

"Professor Wiebe, a philosopher of science, pays serious attention to religious experience. *Visions and Appearances of Jesus* addresses long-standing puzzles: Jesus is believed to have overcome his own death but is no longer to be found easily in our visible world. This book uses recent interviews with people who have had surprising experiences which are difficult to assimilate and marks out the historical ground. It is clearly written and historically sound."

—**Leslie Armour,** Fellow of the Royal Society of Canada, research professor of philosophy at the Dominican University College at Carleton University in Ottawa, professor emeritus at the University of Ottawa. His books include *The Rational and the Real, Being and Idea,* and *Logic and Reality*

"Carefully and with clarity Phillip Wiebe makes the case that historical and contemporary reports of visionary encounters with Jesus are to be taken seriously. Moreover, evaluating these accounts, he suggests the experiences support the claim that, after Easter, Jesus' first followers encountered him in ways that were very real and sometimes resembled the physical encounters of ordinary life. Not only is this book wonderfully well written and easy to read, it makes the important case that religious experience cannot be prematurely dismissed."

—**Graham H. Twelftree,** Charles L. Holman Professor of New Testament and Early Christianity, the School of Divinity, Regent University

"According to anthropological research, ninety percent of people on the planet routinely experience visions and other alternate states of consciousness. In this book, Professor Wiebe summarizes his interviews of thirty subjects who had visions of Jesus and comments on their experiences. He rightly highlights the importance and value of experiential knowledge relative to empirical knowledge. Experiential knowledge points to the existence of an alternate or spiritual reality which is central to these visions. This is beyond the reach of the empirical method. The clear and engaging style of this book recommends it for a wide readership interested in understanding human experience and its ability to know spiritual reality."

—**John J. Pilch,** PhD, lecturer in the Odyssey Program at Johns Hopkins University; previously, a visiting professor of biblical literature at Georgetown University (1993–2011); author of *Visions and Healing in the Acts of the Apostles* (The Liturgical Press, 2004) and *Flights of the Soul* (Wm. B. Eerdmans Publ. Co., 2011)

VISIONS
AND
APPEARANCES
OF
JESUS

VISIONS
AND
APPEARANCES
OF
JESUS

Phillip H. Wiebe

LEAFWOOD
PUBLISHERS

VISIONS AND APPEARANCES OF JESUS

LEAFWOOD
PUBLISHERS

Copyright 2014 by Phillip H. Wiebe

ISBN 978-0-89112-608-9
LCCN 2014005987

Printed in the United States of America

LIBRARY OF CONGRESS CATALOGING-IN-PUBLICATION DATA
Wiebe, Phillip H., 1945-
  Visions and appearances of Jesus / Phillip H. Wiebe.
     pages cm
  Includes bibliographical references.
  ISBN 978-0-89112-608-9
  1. Jesus Christ--Apparitions and miracles. 2. Visions. I. Title.
  BT580.A1W53 2014
  232.9'7--dc23
                                                                        2014005987

Cover design by Marc Whitaker
Interior text design by Sandy Armstrong, Strong Design

For information contact:
Abilene Christian University Press
1626 Campus Court
Abilene, Texas 79601

1-877-816-4455
www.leafwoodpublishers.com

14 15 16 17 18 19 / 7 6 5 4 3 2 1

CONTENTS

PREFACE

I have been interested for fifty years in unusual perceptual experiences in which people report having encountered Jesus Christ himself, but the idea of researching these did not occur to me until the summer of 1988. In the following six years I was privileged to meet people who reported that Jesus had visibly appeared to them. Through strategically placed advertisements and word of mouth, I was able to locate thirty people who were willing to talk to me and let me record our conversations. This book is really their story, and I dedicate it to them, or to their memory in the case of some who have already passed into "the world without end."

Experiences in which people believe they have directly encountered Jesus himself are known by a variety of names—as visions among most Protestants, as apparitions among many Catholics, and sometimes as appearances. The terminology is not fixed for this remarkable phenomenon, and this is appropriate, I think, for the experiences vary so much that settling on a single term is difficult. I will elaborate on some of the interesting variations reported by those who have had what I will call "encounters."

These experiences are widely accepted as having occurred to "the saints" of Christian faith. These are the well-known people who are recognized in the church as having given themselves to lives of prayer, self-denial, acts of mercy, and sometimes martyrdom. Consequently, I preface these twentieth-century experiences with accounts that come down to us from New Testament times.

I published a technical book on this topic titled *Visions of Jesus from New Testament Times to Today* in 1997 with Oxford University Press, and readers who want a "more argumentative" book can consult it. OUP has graciously given me permission to use the stories of present-day people that are presented here in Chapters Four to Seven. I acknowledge, with gratitude, permission to use images shown on Plates in Chapter 8 below: PLATES 8.1 and 8.2: The Holy Shroud Guild; PLATE 8.3: The British Library; PLATE 8.4: Warner Press; PLATE 8.5: John Wesley's House & The Museum of Methodism; PLATE 8.6: The American Psychological Association; PLATE 8.7: Paul Tinsley and family; PLATE 8.8: Osterhus Publishing House.

I also wish to acknowledge the generous assistance of my daughter, Alisa, in reading this manuscript, and to express my thanks to my wife, Shirley, and my son, Jeremy, for their support in this project on the visions of Jesus. I wish my mother had lived to see this book published, for she had a part to play. I dedicate it also to her memory.

INTRODUCTION

Pauline Langlois was brought up in the Catholic Church, but by the time she was in her late teens she didn't go to church or practice her faith, apart from saying the occasional "Our Father" before going to bed. By the age of twenty-three she had been through two divorces and various abusive relationships and had lost the desire to live. She drank to cope with the misery in her life and felt she was becoming the kind of person she hated. She wanted to commit suicide but hesitated to do so because her daughter, who was only five years old, needed her care.

One night as Pauline lay in her bed and thought about ending her life, she became aware of a presence in her bedroom. She wasn't afraid, but she sensed that someone was there even though she could not see anything at first. Then she saw a man standing beside her bed looking at her compassionately. He touched her with his hand to comfort her. She wanted to put out her hand to touch him to see if he was real but was reluctant to do so for fear it would drive him away. So she just lay there, not daring to move. Then he spoke to her. The words she heard in her heart were, "It's okay. I'm going to take care of you. It's all right. I'm taking care of you." She felt great love and joy, and throwing restraint aside, reached out her hand and touched his side. It felt solid to her touch. He stayed there for some time and then just faded from view.

Pauline said the man who appeared wore conventional clothes and was average in height and build, but she could not describe other features of his appearance. His eyes captured her attention, and nothing else was important at that moment. At the time, Pauline did not know who it was that appeared to her, but the desire to take her own life disappeared.

Pauline had not been really convinced about the reality of a spiritual world to this point in her life, but after she had seen the man in her bedroom, a number of bizarre events apparently involving invisible beings convinced her that an evil spirit was trying to scare her: doors would slam behind her; plants would move across the table; water taps would switch on and off; music would come from the corners of the rooms; and various objects of furniture would move on their own across the floor. At first she wondered if she had gone crazy, but when members of her extended family witnessed these events as well, she knew there must be some other explanation.

Pauline went to several priests for help. One gave her holy water to sprinkle on her home, as well as on her daughter, whose safety she was worried about, but this did not help. Pauline finally traveled from Burnaby, British Columbia, where she was living at the time, to her childhood home in Sudbury, Ontario, to consult the family priest. When he heard about the troubling events, he instructed her to take "the Good Spirit" with her to confront them. She asked him where the Good Spirit could be found, and he answered, "He is here in this room. Just take him with you!" She replied, "Okay, Good Spirit. Let's go!" and returned to Burnaby.

Thereafter, each time a bizarre event took place, she would say something like, "Okay, Good Spirit, that's what I want you to get rid of." Eventually, all of the frightening events disappeared. During these months she also began attending a prayer and Bible study group near her home.

A short while after the frightening events stopped, she had another experience that made her want to commit suicide. She did not describe details of the experience to me, except to suggest it involved physical assault. She acquired the pills she needed to take her life, but the thought came to her that she should first pray. She prayed, "God, if there is a God, if you are really there, I need you now." Pauline says she felt the same presence enter the room that had been there at the first experience. He said to her, "I'm so happy to see you," and she felt the same love that she had felt the first time. Although Pauline saw nothing the second time, she is convinced that the presence on this occasion, as well as the first, was Jesus.

Pauline had another experience several years later in which Jesus appeared in the sky above her head. She saw him from the waist up, surrounded by a very bright cloud. His form was so large that it filled the sky. Pauline described this third experience as a vision, but she did not use that term to describe the first encounter, saying that experience "was very different. It was alive. It was like you and me [now talking together]. It was like a real man standing right there. It was a man, not a spirit."

These events were life-changing for Pauline, and when I met her about nine years later, she, her husband, and four children were operating a small farm near Sudbury.

Appearance to Mary Magdalene

According to several ancient traditions preserved in the New Testament, Mary Magdalene was the first person to whom Jesus appeared after his resurrection. We might think that he would have appeared first to one of his closest disciples, perhaps Peter or John, especially because the testimony of women was not given much weight in Jewish Palestine of the first century. However, Jesus often seems to have acted contrary to others' expectations of him.

Mary is described as having been "possessed by seven devils" before Jesus brought healing and peace to her life. The exact meaning behind being "possessed by devils" is unclear, but Mary's background does not appear to make her a very credible witness. In spite of this, however, she was chosen to be the first to encounter Jesus alive after his passion. Pauline Langlois's story suggests that people still have encounters with dark forces that seek their destruction, but—like Mary—Pauline experienced freedom from these forces through the intervention of Jesus.

Like Pauline, Mary did not recognize Jesus when he first appeared to her after his resurrection. Mary had gone to Jesus' grave to complete the burial process that had been interrupted by the Sabbath but found it empty. She saw someone she took to be the gardener and asked him where Jesus' body had been taken. When the man spoke her name, Mary knew he was not the gardener but the risen Lord. She fell at his feet, evidently making some move to touch him in this act of worship. He did not allow it, however. We might marvel at Mary's bold attempt to grasp him with her hands, but this is a natural move people often make in an effort to establish that the things we see, or seem to see, are "really real." Pauline Langlois did the same.

Encounters of this kind, also known as visions or apparitions, are never an end in themselves. Some message is typically conveyed by the experience, although this message is not always spoken. In

Mary's case, the message Jesus gave was that he was alive and that she should tell his disciples. In Pauline's case, the message was that she was loved and that someone was looking after her. The importance of the message to Pauline can be seen by how frequently it, or something similar, is conveyed in personal encounters with a being that people believe is the risen Christ.

Personal Interest in Direct Encounters

My interest in the subject of direct encounters was kindled in 1965 by a report of an appearance of Jesus to a whole congregation in a church in Oakland, California—an appearance reportedly filmed. I will describe the circumstances surrounding this event in Chapter Seven. Several reports that came my way in the next seven or eight years persuaded me that the phenomenon deserved closer scrutiny.

In 1970, when I was a student at the University of Adelaide in South Australia, I heard a professor of engineering from India relate his two visions of Jesus. In each he was called to be a disciple, and after the second he answered the call. This experience caught my attention at the time because the dominant religious influence in his life had been Hinduism, not Christianity, so the experience did not seem to fit with the common belief that only Christians have visions of Jesus. Of course, Christianity has been in India for a very long time, so the influences upon this professor might have been subconscious. I did not speak directly with him about his experiences.

The third incident is of a more personal kind, as it involves an encounter with Jesus linked to my mother. My parents were involved in pastoral work for most of their lives, and the stresses that can go with this kind of vocation brought about a mental breakdown in my mother. In her mid-forties, she became depressed and in need of medical care. I did not really appreciate the extent of her illness at the time, for I was in my early teens and very much caught up with my own interests. Although she recovered significantly with rest and my father's taking a break from pastoral work, she received a remarkable healing about fifteen years after her breakdown. She told me that after her own healing she would often experience a tingling sensation in her arms and hands as she prayed for others in need. On one occasion, a friend for whom Mother prayed afterward reported that she had seen Jesus standing beside my mother. Mother saw nothing but was humbled and awestruck by the incident. It happened in 1971 or 1972, when I was still in Adelaide, and I did not hear about her vision until I returned to my home in Canada in the latter part of 1972. Mother did not speak of it often and would only do so if she was sure her story would not be met with ridicule. She died years before the research on this book began.

Visions and apparitions in general, let alone such experiences of Jesus, raise many questions. We might wonder if direct encounters with a being considered to be the risen Christ might be similar to those recorded in the New Testament and whether they support the extraordinary Christian claim that Jesus was resurrected. We might also wonder if science can explain these strange perceptual events and what relation might exist between science and religion when it comes to visions. These are some of the questions I will address in this book.

The claim that visions of Jesus still occur is not in doubt. What these visions signify, however, is a matter of dispute. That such visions are significant—not least for those who experience them—is undeniable.

CHAPTER 1

NEW TESTAMENT AND APOCRYPHAL APPEARANCES

At the center of the Christian faith is the remarkable claim that Jesus Christ came back to life, and not merely in the form that marked his human life but in an immortal form. Although other religions make wonderful claims about their founders, no other faith depends at the very core of its existence upon such an extraordinary claim. The Christian conviction that Jesus was God in human form, participating in human suffering and death and somehow overcoming them, would hardly be believable if he had not also been brought back to life.

Although the church sometimes presents the resurrection of Jesus as "an article of faith" for which evidence should not be sought, this is not how most of the New Testament writers themselves approach it. Saint Paul, for example, explicitly advances evidence for the resurrection in one of his letters to the Corinthians. Saint John also explains to his readers that his accounts of various experiences, including appearances of Jesus after his death, are evidence for central Christian beliefs.

Although many Christians appear to accept the resurrection on the authority of either the church or the Bible, people of other faiths or of no religious leanings understandably have difficulty with the claim that someone came back to life approximately 2,000 years ago. Defenders of Christian faith have addressed this central doctrine with much vigor and ingenuity, especially as other scholars have turned their critical attention to the New Testament and have questioned its historical accuracy. Perhaps no claim in Christian faith has been subject to more scrutiny from scholars in the last 200 years than the resurrection. The issue seems to be at a stalemate in Western culture, with most Christians continuing to defend its authenticity, while their academic critics continue to advance serious objections.

One popular response to stalemates over religion is to treat those disputed claims as open for individual interpretation. Implicit in this response is the idea that differences over religion cannot be settled in a satisfactory way and that, because both views are equally legitimate, those who dispute such matters should simply go their separate ways. An analogy is sometimes drawn with seemingly insoluble moral disputes, in which competing views about matters of value are considered to have equal merit, perhaps on the basis that all parties to a dispute sincerely hold to or thoughtfully embrace their positions. However, the claim that a man came back to life nearly two millennia ago is not only a religious one, but also a historical one, and so seems to be different from insoluble religious or moral claims that cannot have significant evidence advanced in favor of or against them.

I am not asserting that historical claims have no "relativism" about them, for such claims might be described differently by people from various cultures and languages, and people from different cultures might differ in the features of events that they chose to observe or report. History, however, makes claims about past events deemed to be "real," even though these might be rather vaguely described or incompletely sketched. The claim that Jesus of Nazareth came back to life after having been killed by the Romans is a historical claim for which a person can plausibly ask for evidence, regardless of what some people might teach about "taking everything on faith." The early church writers also regarded the resurrection as something for which evidence could be displayed.

The Evidence Required of a Resurrection

What evidence would need to be advanced, we might ask, in order to plausibly assert that someone actually came back to life? In order to respond to this question without making assumptions about the resurrection of Jesus, we might ask the question about someone else who is also well-known to history. What evidence, for example, would need to be put forward in order to defend the claim that former British Prime Minister Winston Churchill came back to life? The answer seems to be that evidence would be needed to support three distinct claims.

A Death

The first is evidence that Churchill actually died and that reports of his death were not fraudulent or somehow mistaken. This question can become quite complex when it focuses on international figures such as Churchill who direct a nation in the time of war and consequently are targets of terrorist attacks as Churchill was. However, he clearly survived the war and evidently died of natural causes in 1965. No doubt has ever been expressed about reports of Churchill's death, unlike, for example, the suspicion that arose concerning the death of U.S. President John F. Kennedy, who was assassinated in 1963. Moreover, even if the report of Churchill's death in 1965 was a huge hoax, we might reasonably expect that he is now dead, given that he was born in 1874 and few European people in his time lived beyond 100 years. The claim that Churchill actually died is not only beyond reasonable doubt, but is also beyond any doubt at all.

A Reappearance

The second claim for which we could legitimately demand evidence is that Churchill has been seen alive after his death and that the person who is considered to be the resurrected Winston Churchill is indeed the person he is taken to be. Implicit in this demand is ensuring that Winston did not have a cousin or a twin brother who looked a lot like him, which raises an issue that is more complex than it appears. Children of prominent and noble families such as Churchill's are sometimes unaware of the existence of siblings and cousins, given the secret infidelities that these social classes have sometimes pursued. Moreover, men who closely resembled Churchill were used by the British intelligence to foil plots on his life. Consequently, mistakes about identity are conceivable among those who would contend that they actually saw Churchill alive after his incontestable death.

Another curious and contentious issue arises in connection with satisfying this second condition for plausibly asserting that someone has come back to life. I am thinking here about alleged apparitions of the dead, which are significantly doubted by many people. If Churchill really died and then was seen after his death, we could plausibly assert that he had been resurrected only if we were sure that Churchill himself had been seen, not merely the "ghost" of Churchill. Of course, if ghosts do not exist, then this condition does not have to be met. However, another issue now arises, and that has to do with the possibility that someone reporting a sighting of Churchill has seen a hallucination, as this is commonly interpreted, rather than a Churchill himself.

A Missing Corpse

These remarks lead naturally to the third condition that needs to be met in order to argue plausibly that someone has come back from death, which is that the corpse of the dead person no longer exists. If Churchill has truly come back to life, we would expect to find no remains of his corpse in his tomb in Bladon, England. Moreover, we would expect not to find his corpse in any tomb at all, no matter where we looked. If someone has truly been brought back to life from death, his or her corpse would not exist *anywhere*. The terms set out in this condition are extremely difficult to satisfy, of course, but this is what coming back to life actually involves.

These three conditions obviously do not consider the consequences of Churchill's coming back to life, but they constitute the absolute minimum evidence that would need to be presented in order to make the claim of resurrection plausible.

The Extraordinary Resurrection

Any claim that a dead person has returned to life is highly unusual, of course, and the resurrection of Jesus is generally considered to be different even from these other accounts, for Jesus is said to have been raised from death as an immortal being. Unlike Jesus, no "ordinary" person said to have come back to life has been considered to have become immortal. Because of the extraordinary nature exhibited by the resurrected Jesus, I prefer to describe other cases of a dead person returning to life as "resuscitations" and restrict the term "resurrection" to the kind of life now exhibited by Jesus. My preference does not quite conform to common usage, however, as people who have lost their breath or their pulse are often said to have been resuscitated when their lungs and heart begin functioning properly again, even if they were not "dead" in any well-established sense of this term.[1]

Setting aside for now the assertion that Jesus was raised immortal, the three conditions I outlined above would need to be satisfied in order to assert plausibly that Jesus was resurrected at all. We would need to show, first, that Jesus actually died as a result of crucifixion and was not merely comatose when placed in the sepulcher; second, that he was seen alive after his death; and third, that his corpse did not exist since he was once again alive. Few biblical critics or theologians now claim that Jesus did not really die from crucifixion and other terrors associated with it, although such a position seems to have been popular among critics of orthodox Christian faith in the nineteenth century. However, the second and third conditions are more contentious today.

Importance of Appearances

We can now see how the appearances of Jesus after his death by crucifixion significantly affect the claim that he was resurrected. Although we can imagine a situation in which a person came back to life but was never seen afterward, the claim of this person's return to life would lack one crucial piece of evidence and thus would not be worthy of serious consideration. A plausible claim to resurrection is dependent upon reliable reports that the resurrected person was seen alive again after death.

In a later chapter, I will discuss the third condition—a missing corpse—in more detail. But in this book, I will focus on perceptual experiences in which people report that Jesus *appeared*, or was *encountered*, or was seen in a *vision*, or was seen as an *apparition*. I will discuss these frequently used terms later, in connection with some specific accounts of contemporary experiences.

The appearances of Jesus are particularly important in defending the resurrection, in part because no one actually saw the dead body of Jesus come back to life. In the Gospels we find accounts of

Jesus raising various people from the dead, such as the one in Luke 7, in which Jesus interrupted the burial procession for a widow's son and brought the young man back to life. The account says the young man came back to life when Jesus touched his coffin. No possible doubt could have existed about *who* came back to life, at least not for the people who witnessed the incident, for they would have seen a corpse become a living person.

But the resurrection of Jesus took place at a time when no one was around. The tomb in which he had been placed was found empty, but this is not enough evidence to establish that someone was resurrected. The appearances of Jesus were needed to help clinch the matter, and they evidently did for the early believers.

Collateral Evidence

Some defenders of the resurrection argue that the strongest evidence comes from the changed attitude of Jesus' disciples—from sorrow over his death to joy at hearing he had come back to life—and the emergence of the Christian Church. Neither of these is considered to be explainable on any basis other than Jesus' returning to life.

However, I consider these to be collateral evidence, not primary evidence, and I base my opinion on what might happen in the hypothetical resuscitation of Churchill. If he came back to life and resumed his place in British public life, we might expect that Churchill's friends would be delighted at the discovery that he somehow cheated death, and we also could expect that his foes would be upset. These are more incidental consequences of Churchill's coming back to life, however, and would presuppose that Churchill's grave was empty and that he had been seen alive after his death. The more crucial conditions for plausibly claiming that Churchill has come back to life are the three conditions I have identified. However, because the supposed effects of his resuscitation on his friends and enemies are plausible consequences, they should be counted as contributing some evidence.

If Churchill had come back to life, we can easily imagine a society dedicated to studying his books and speeches would emerge. This would be comparable to the emergence of the Christian Church several millennia ago, but because Churchill's resuscitation would have occurred quite recently, we could hardly expect that "Churchill societies" would have had the time to be established all over the world. While the formation of Churchill societies could be evidence that he had been resuscitated, such societies would only provide collateral evidence because they could exist for reasons other than Churchill's resuscitation. The fact that Churchill wrote insightful books and gave inspiring speeches might be sufficient reason for such study groups, or *the mere belief* that he had been resuscitated (perhaps because his ghost had been observed) could provide a basis for the establishment of such societies.

This point about collateral evidence is reinforced by realizing that the existence of significant religious movements is seldom considered as evidence verifying the extraordinary claims of the movements' founders. Consider the claims of Joseph Smith, who founded the Church of Latter-Day Saints about two centuries ago. The fact that this church now numbers about eleven million hardly provides a compelling basis to embrace the historicity of Joseph Smith's claim that he found gold plates on which *The Book of Mormon* was written. We might consider the rise of that movement as collateral evidence for his account, but Smith's remarkable claim needs to be more directly supported to be plausible.

I conclude that the changed attitude of Jesus' disciples and the rise of the Christian Church are collateral to the primary evidence I mentioned, which includes appearances of Jesus to his followers after his death.

Appearances and Visions of Jesus

The New Testament itself never describes the resurrection of Jesus in any detail, but an apocryphal book comes close. The apocryphal books, like the books of the New Testament, are texts that circulated in the early church, but their authority for establishing fundamental beliefs and doctrines was not accepted by the majority of its leaders. The apocryphal Gospel of Peter tells a story of two men coming down from heaven in great brightness, opening the tomb in which Jesus was buried, and helping him to walk out. As the three men left the tomb, a cross is said to have followed them. This story makes the resurrected Jesus seem like a weakling, and not the Lord of Christian faith who has authority over all things in heaven and on earth. For some reason, we have not been given an authoritative description of the resurrection itself. But we have a number of accounts of appearances to his disciples and followers.

The New Testament contains nearly two dozen accounts of appearances and visions of Jesus. Theologians and biblical scholars usually describe the encounters with Jesus after his resurrection but before his ascension as *appearances*, reserving the term *visions* to describe the encounters after his ascension. Tradition has considered Jesus' appearances to be as physical and as real in character as the appearances of any normal living person. Visions, however, have been widely considered as highly subjective and fleeting, with no claim to revealing things that exist. This distinction is not found in Scripture, however, and does not seem to square with Paul's interpretation of the various ways Jesus was encountered after the ascension. One of these encounters was Paul's own dramatic conversion experience, which occurred some years after the ascension.

Scholars believe that the earliest New Testament text referring to the resurrection and various appearances that provide evidence of it is 1 Corinthians 15, where Saint Paul lists six groups or individuals to whom Jesus appeared:

- Peter the apostle
- The twelve disciples
- More than 500 brethren at once
- James the apostle
- All the apostles, and
- Paul himself

We have to go to the Gospels and to Acts of the Apostles, written by Saint Luke, for more details of some of these experiences since Paul does not give us any. Paul's famous encounter on the road to Damascus is described three times in Acts, which gives us some idea of how important it was considered to be, at least by Luke. Paul himself tells us that it was this encounter that was the source for his apostolic ministry.

Although many theologians say the ascension marks the moment the appearances of Jesus stopped and the visions of Jesus began, Paul's reference to the 500 brethren seems to be an experience that took place after the ascension because at Pentecost, which took place a few days after the ascension, only 120 followers are said to have been gathered in the upper room to receive the gift of the Holy Spirit. This number is widely considered an estimate of the number of disciples at the time, and if accurate, Jesus' appearance to the 500 believers could hardly have occurred before the ascension. Paul, however, labels the experience as an appearance, not as a vision.

Of course, it is possible that Jesus appeared to a mixed group of disciples and the general public numbering about 500. However, the New Testament pattern indicates he appeared only to followers, not the general public. Moreover, if he had appeared to the general public, we might reasonably expect that some evidence of this appearance would have been preserved in some source other than the canonical gospels, such as a public record of significant events in the life of the nation like that written in the first century by Josephus.

Although we cannot definitely say when the appearance to the 500 took place, we know that Paul's own experience occurred after the ascension. This means that Paul did not distinguish appearances from visions in the way that tradition has done. This point is important when we consider the experiences of people living today. Perhaps these experiences should not be described simply as visions in an effort to discredit their significance. Perhaps some of them should even be accorded the authority and significance that theologians have given to appearances. In this age when many critics of Christianity are skeptical of crucial claims about Jesus, some contemporary experiences possibly add to the evidence of the resurrection.

Another interesting feature of Paul's list is that it includes at least three encounters in which more than a single person encountered the risen Christ (Paul's experience is ambiguous). In other words, these encounters were public, and public experiences powerfully attest to the fact that an object seen by many is real. I am not insisting that private experiences are not encounters of reality, but skeptical arguments are much harder to refute when those experiences are not shared. As we shall see in later chapters, modern encounters involve both public and private experiences.

Appearances in the Gospels

The Gospel of Mark is widely considered to have been the earliest of the gospels, even though it does not appear first in the New Testament. The ending of this gospel has long been in dispute, and several endings can be found in ancient manuscripts. Older Bibles include a long ending that includes brief accounts of three appearances: to Mary Magdalene, who once anointed the feet of Jesus with expensive perfume; to two people walking in the country; and to the eleven disciples who remained in Jerusalem after the death of Jesus. (The twelfth disciple, Judas Iscariot, betrayed Jesus and then committed suicide at the time of the crucifixion.)

The short ending of Mark contains no mention of appearances at all, and ends with an account of the women leaving the grave of Jesus in fright. This ending has seemed incomplete to many theologians, who have expressed misgiving about a gospel that ends on a negative note and includes no accounts of appearances. But we do not know more about the ending of this gospel. The fact that Matthew and Luke resemble Mark in general ways, and have several accounts of appearances after the resurrection, suggests that Mark might have originally included several as well. In any case, we find accounts in other gospels that shed light on Paul's important list of appearances.

The Gospel of Matthew tells the story of an angel descending from heaven to roll back the stone over the opening to the sepulcher in which the dead body of Jesus had been placed. The angel told Mary Magdalene and another Mary, who had come to see the sepulcher, that Jesus had risen, and instructed them to tell the disciples the news. As the women left the tomb, Jesus met them. They responded by taking hold of his feet and worshipping him. He responds with, "Do not be afraid; go and tell my brethren to go to Galilee, and there they will see me."

Matthew concludes with an account of the eleven disciples going north of Jerusalem to Galilee as they had been directed. When Jesus met them there, they worshipped him, and he then commissioned them with these words: "Go therefore and make disciples of all nations, baptizing them in the name of the Father and of the Son and of the Holy Spirit."

Paul's reference to the twelve disciples seeing Jesus is enigmatic. He could be referring to the experience described by Matthew, using the expression "the twelve" somewhat loosely to refer to the original band of disciples without Judas Iscariot. Another possibility is that other disciples were there when Jesus ascended, but Matthew did not mention them. In Acts we read how the eleven disciples drew lots and selected Saint Matthias to take the place of Judas. One of the requirements Matthias had to satisfy was being a witness to the resurrection. Perhaps he was present when Jesus ascended into heaven, and maybe Paul included him when he spoke about Jesus appearing to the twelve disciples. We who live in this scientific age sometimes demand a precision of the writers of Scripture that they would not have expected of one another. This point is important to keep in mind when we find puzzling differences in seemingly parallel accounts.

Like Matthew, The Gospel of Luke gives accounts of only two appearances. Someone named Cleopas and an unidentified man experience the first encounter with Jesus as they walked the seven miles from Jerusalem to Emmaus. Many have thought that the second person was Saint Peter. This would explain Paul's explicit reference to Jesus appearing to Peter. Luke says that as the three walked along they talked about the crucifixion of Jesus, and even the rumor that Jesus had been resurrected. But the two disciples did not recognize their companion until they sat down to eat in Emmaus. Luke describes it as follows: "When he was at table with them, he took the bread and blessed, and broke it, and gave it to them. And their eyes were opened and they recognized him; and he vanished out of their sight." The long ending of Mark gives a very brief description of this encounter, saying only, "He appeared in another form to two of them as they were walking into the country."

The idea that Jesus appeared in different forms has not been widely considered in Christian thought, in spite of the remark just quoted. He is generally considered to have always appeared with the signs of crucifixion in his hands and feet, and the wound in his side. Consequently, appearances not having these features have even been considered diabolical counterfeits. Mark and Luke appear to be describing the same walk in the country, but whereas Luke says the disciples were prevented from recognizing Jesus, Mark says Jesus appeared in a different form.

Luke then relates how these two disciples returned that same night to Jerusalem to tell the eleven disciples what they had seen. As they told their story, "Jesus himself stood among them." This frightened the gathered disciples, for they supposed that they saw a spirit. But Jesus calmed them, inviting them to touch him and convince themselves that he was not a spirit. To give further proof of his having a substantial body, he ate the piece of broiled fish that they gave him. This incident is interesting, for it shows that the question of whether the resurrected Jesus was only a disembodied spirit was asked even in the first century. Moreover, Jesus allowed the issue to be settled by first-hand evidence—he showed that he was real and substantial, even though his new body was immortal.

Luke concludes with Jesus' leading his disciples to nearby Bethany, commissioning them to preach, and parting from them, implying that the ascension into heaven took place in Bethany. In Saint Matthew's gospel, the ascension takes place in Galilee. This apparent discrepancy has been the subject of much controversy, and several approaches can be used when examining this and other differing accounts. I will examine how modern experiences shed some light on the New Testament accounts of encounters with Christ, and—although they do not solve all problems of interpretation— these experiences suggest that we are dealing with mysteries that take us into a "world" beyond the scope of normal human experience.

The Gospel of John also gives an account of an appearance to Mary Magdalene on the morning of the resurrection, but in this account she is not allowed to touch him because he has not yet ascended. That very day Jesus appeared to most of his disciples. "Doubting Thomas" was not present at this appearance, however, and when told about it, he exclaimed, "Unless I see in his hands the print of the nails, and place my finger in the mark of the nails, and place my hand in his side, I will not believe." Eight days later, Saint Thomas was satisfied, when, for the second time, Jesus appeared in a room whose doors were shut. Jesus said to Thomas, "Put your finger here, and see my hands; and put out your hand, and place it in my side; do not be faithless, but believing." Thomas responded, "My Lord and my God."

These incidents are interesting for several reasons. They indicate that Jesus can appear with the stigmata—that is, the marks of crucifixion in his hands, feet, and side. Nothing in the accounts indicates he was always seen with the stigmata, but Jesus is said to have allowed Thomas on this occasion to examine the wounds for himself. In modern encounters, Jesus is often seen without the stigmata, a fact that troubles some people. But we do not know how often Jesus was seen with the stigmata in the original appearances.

The incidents in John are also interesting because they imply that the ascension took place in the first eight days after the resurrection. Jesus does not allow Mary Magdalene to touch him on the day of the resurrection because he had not yet ascended to his Father, but he does not object to Thomas's touching him eight days later, suggesting that the ascension took place within those eight days. But Luke's account of the ascension in Acts puts this event forty days after the resurrection.

One explanation for the apparent discrepancy is that Jesus moved freely between earth and heaven (the "realm" of his Father) during the forty days in question, and did not allow Mary to touch him because he had just been resurrected. By the time Thomas

31

wanted to touch him in order to examine his wounds, Jesus had already been with his Father. The official ascension after forty days indicated to his disciples that they could no longer depend on his physical presence as they had experienced it. Instead, they were to receive and be led by the Holy Spirit, which was given at Pentecost.

The fourth appearance described by John takes place at the Sea of Galilee, and he devotes a whole chapter to it. Seven disciples were in a fishing boat on this occasion when they saw someone they did not recognize on the shore. This stranger instructed them to cast their net on the right side of the boat, and when they did, they caught so many fish they were hardly able to haul them in. Peter realized at that moment that it was Jesus who stood on the shore, already having prepared a meal of baked fish and bread. John's account continues with a poignant conversation between Peter and Jesus in which Peter, who had denied knowing Jesus at the trial before his crucifixion, expresses his love and devotion for Jesus.

I have briefly described all of the accounts of appearances found in the gospels; some of them describe the same incidents with slight variations in details. Establishing a definite list of incidents is difficult. The brief descriptions given above present several problems for biblical interpretation, including:

- Determining the number of the appearances
- Determining the order of the appearances
- Identifying the places where the appearances occurred
- Identifying the persons to whom Jesus appeared
- Establishing the timing of the ascension
- Establishing whether all the appearances occurred before the ascension
- Establishing the nature of the resurrection body

- Determining the differences, if any, between the appearances and the visions of Jesus

Scholars continue to debate these issues, and many ingenious ideas have been put forward in recent decades in order to solve various problems. The traditional view of the Christian Church that the resurrection can be considered a concrete, physical event is under scrutiny in academic circles, but it is still widely supported in the church. I believe that contemporary experiences support the claim that Jesus was originally encountered in ways that were very real, and that these encounters sometimes resemble the physical encounters we are familiar with in ordinary life.

New Testament Visions of Jesus

The most significant recorded encounter with Jesus after his ascension is the experience that took place at Paul's conversion on the way to Damascus. Three similar accounts of Paul's experience are given in Acts. All accounts agree that a light shone from heaven, and that someone identifying himself as Jesus spoke to Paul. But the accounts differ on details such as the content of the message, whether Paul was the only one to fall to the ground, and whether Paul's companions also heard the voice and saw the light. These differences are slight, however, and resemble those typically encountered when a single event is described several times. The insignificant differences help to establish the credibility of what is described because they show that Luke was not concerned about "editing" his accounts so that every detail would match.

The three accounts Luke gives us are important in one respect, for each notes that everyone present experienced a different effect of the encounter with Christ, indicating that the experience was not merely subjective but belonged to the domain of public events. Some scholars would classify this event as an appearance, not a vision, and this seems to be the way in which Paul himself understood his experience.

More Visions of Paul

Several other visions of Jesus are attributed to Paul. He had a trance experience just after returning to Jerusalem following his conversion in which Jesus warned him to leave Jerusalem because his life was in danger. However, Luke does not provide further details in Acts about the nature of the trance. Paul also had a vision in Corinth, in which he was encouraged to keep on with his preaching. In a fourth experience, Jesus "stood by" Paul in the night to comfort him because of his persecutors in Jerusalem, and to inform him that he would be going to Rome. Although the last of these descriptions is very brief, it presents the encounter as taking place on earth. In some visions, the recipient seems to enter or see into heaven, but in others Jesus seems to come to people on earth.

We might think that Paul had more than enough encounters with the risen Christ, but yet another vision is associated with his conversion. In Acts, Luke describes how a disciple named Ananias was instructed by Jesus in a vision to find Paul, who had been blinded in the encounter on the road to Damascus, and lay hands on him so that he might receive his sight. In light of all these extraordinary events, we should not be surprised to read in Paul's letters that he felt his call into apostolic ministry came from Christ himself and was consequently authentic. Some people today trace their calling into Christian ministry to a personal appearance of Jesus, but this clearly is not the experience of most ministers. Neither does this experience necessarily demonstrate the reality of such a calling to those who experience an appearance. However, I do not think that the experience, when it does occur, is trivial. Those to whom Jesus appears probably still need to search for their place in the world, as well as in the church, as much as any Christian who makes a serious commitment but has no extraordinary experience.

Visions of Others

Luke reports in Acts that Saint Stephen saw a vision of Jesus as he was being stoned to death. In Acts 7:8, Luke says that Stephen "gazed into heaven and saw the glory of God, and Jesus standing at the right hand of God." No more detail is given about this experience, and Luke does not say whether bystanders could see what Stephen described, but it is generally assumed that he was the only one who could see Jesus. This is the earliest of the visions of Jesus in which someone is described as seeing into heaven.

Revelation is well-known for its reports of dramatic and mysterious visions. It opens with a detailed account of a vision of Jesus, experienced by someone named John. Many modern scholars question whether the writer was the apostle John, primarily because the book's style is different from the Gospel of John. In Revelation, Jesus is seen with hair as white as wool or snow, eyes like a flame of fire, feet like fire, and a face shining like the sun in full strength. His voice is described as having the sound of many waters, and a flame issues out of his mouth; in his right hand, he holds seven stars.

This is the only detailed description of Jesus found in the New Testament, which is curious, as many people have wondered what he looked like and what his original disciples actually saw. We do not think, however, that they saw what the author of Revelation describes, for this description is considered to be symbolic. No authoritative account of Jesus' actual appearance has come to us from the early writings. The historian Eusebius, writing in the fourth century, says a statue depicting Jesus' healing someone stood in Philippi, but he does not say whether the likeness was accurate or how Jesus appeared in real life. I will address this issue further elsewhere.

Visions of Jesus in the Apocrypha

A sizable number of experiences are recounted in the New Testament Apocrypha. Much of this literature is attributed to the Christian Gnostics, who claimed they had special knowledge of spiritual matters and could interpret the scriptures by means of mystical experience. Many Gnostics doubted the *physical* reality of the resurrected Jesus and so have been viewed as less than orthodox by those who gave Christianity its distinctive dogmas. Gnostics claim that spiritual beings have much greater value than physical ones, which is a view that can be traced back to Plato and other Greek philosophers. Willis Barnstone, editor of a recent collection of ancient books under the title *The Other Bible*, remarks that if the Gnostic Valentinus had become the pope, the content of the New Testament, which was established authoritatively in 397 in a church council in Carthage, would have looked rather different than the one we know today.[2] How much authority should be given to the literature valued by the Gnostics? While these books are not used within Christendom to defend its doctrines, their accounts of visions or apparitions in which Jesus was supposedly seen could be based on actual experiences.

In the book Acts of Peter, a story recounts a vision of Jesus that Peter had on the day his daughter was born. Jesus is said to have informed him then that his daughter would do harm to many people if she were healthy. Peter then describes how she became paralyzed at ten years of age, as she was about to be married, and how this resulted in her remaining a virgin all her life. At one point in the story, those who know about his power to heal challenge Peter to demonstrate his ability on his daughter. He does so successfully, but a few minutes later she returns to her paralytic condition in order to fulfill a higher calling. The story gives expression to the value placed on sexual continence by the early Christians, and the vision of Jesus helps to reinforce the point.

A significant part of Acts of Peter is a description of Peter's conflict with Simon Magus, a Gnostic magician. The text describes a vision of Jesus in which the dramatic events involving Simon were foretold. Although the vision took place as night came on, the text notes that Peter was awake and also describes Jesus as smiling and robed in splendor, which are the types of details the biblical accounts of appearances do not supply. The style of the narratives in this second-century book also differ noticeably from the style found in the Gospels.

Encounters of Thomas

Acts of Thomas tells of the events that led to Thomas's going to India to preach the gospel. When the apostles were still in Jerusalem, they drew lots to determine where they would travel. According to the lot, India fell to Thomas, but he did not want to go. Jesus then appeared to him and told him to go, but even this did not convince Thomas. The story goes that a merchant from India was in Jerusalem wanting to buy a carpenter to take back to India. Jesus met the merchant in the marketplace and sold Thomas to the merchant, writing out the appropriate deed of sale. Then Jesus brought him Thomas, who had no choice but to go to India, for he acknowledged that he was the slave of Jesus.

The story continues with an event in India where Jesus appeared to a bridal couple and convinced them to abstain from sexual intercourse. In this encounter, he appeared to them first in the likeness of Thomas. This story is interesting for various reasons. It reveals the value of chastity in early Christian thought, but it also presents the encounters as taking place in various forms. The first encounter is a vision at night, the details of which are not given. The second encounter involves Jesus interacting as an ordinary man with the carpenter and Thomas. The third involves Jesus coming in disguise.

Evaluating the apocryphal accounts is not an easy task. Long familiarity with the established New Testament books perhaps contributes to doubts about the value of the apocryphal books, and we might be inclined to dismiss them as completely fanciful. But we also have to consider the possibility that some elements might be rooted in actual experience. Another fact on which we do well to reflect is that the ministry of Thomas described in this apocryphal book is widely accepted—Christianity took root in India in antiquity and is associated with Thomas. I am not suggesting that the apocryphal books should be used along with the canonical New Testament texts to establish doctrine, but we should consider the possibility that some authentic experiences might be included in them.

Experiences of Other Apostles

The Apocryphon of James describes an appearance of Jesus to the twelve disciples 550 days after his resurrection. In this incident, James and Peter are drawn aside for special instruction, and after Jesus leaves them, these two disciples "send their spirits to heaven" to hear and see various sights, including angels in worship. This book touches on practices widely questioned in Christendom, including "soul travel" or "astral travel," and attempts to enter the heavenly domains by such activities. Paul is thought by some theologians to condemn such practices in his letter to the Colossian Christians, where believers supposedly capable of such feats considered themselves better than others who could not.

The Epistula Apostolorum describes an appearance to the eleven disciples strikingly similar to accounts found in the Gospels. The disciples are described as doubtful about what they see when Jesus appears. To reassure them of his identity, Jesus invites Peter to put his finger in the nail print in his hands, Thomas to put his hand in Jesus' side, and Andrew to verify that Jesus' footstep leaves an imprint in the ground. The text continues: "For it is written in the prophet, 'But a ghost, or demon, leaves no print on the ground.'"[3] This account is similar to one in Luke in which Jesus allows his disciples to touch him in order to assure themselves that his resurrection body was real and physical. No canonical gospel includes a "footprint test," however.

The Letter of Peter to Philip refers to a vision of Jesus so bright that a mountain was illuminated by it. The vision was accompanied by a voice that said, "Hear my words, that I may send you! Why do you seek after me? I am Jesus Christ, who is with you for ever."[4] Another early apocryphal book is the Gospel of Mary, in which Jesus informs Mary that a person's understanding sees a vision, not a person's soul or spirit. Here we have a rare early attempt to give an explanation of the mechanism by which visions occur. The three-part division of the "person" here into soul, spirit, and understanding anticipates the influential view of visions articulated in the fifth century by Saint Augustine. He argued that corporeal visions involve the outer senses such as eyes and ears, that imaginative visions bypass the outer senses and influence the imagination directly, and that intellectual visions involve neither the outer senses nor the imaginative powers of a person but only the intellect. The last of these is perhaps the most difficult to understand, and to illustrate intellectual vision Augustine mentions the experience of coming to understand the character of self-giving love (agape). We would not call this a vision today, but Augustine must have understood insight into spiritual and moral matters that involve no images of any kind to be comparable to experiences in which objects or images appeared.

Augustine gives the impression that the difference between a corporeal vision and an imaginative vision would be easy to spot.

He tells the story of a peasant who related his visionary experience but was considered by Augustine to be "too simple" to determine "whether it was a body or the image of a body" that appeared.[5] Although Augustine leaves the impression that more discerning individuals could tell the difference, he does not indicate how. Augustine did not think that visions of Jesus in which people used their eyes (corporeal visions) actually required Jesus to be present, maintaining that Jesus is in heaven, and thus cannot be seen in an ordinary way. According to Augustine, when Jesus seems to appear to people, even before their open eyes, this is because angels are producing images of him. Using this interpretation, the church has been able to accept that visions of Jesus are "authentic," in some sense of the term, and to continue to teach that he is in heaven, unavailable for viewing in any ordinary sense.

The Death of Mary

One of the most significant encounters with Jesus after his resurrection is said to have taken place at the time of the death of his mother, Mary. Several accounts of this event have come down to us, attributed either to Saint John or Saint James, the brother (or stepbrother) of Jesus. One account is in Greek, and two are in Latin, and although these agree on the main facts of the event, they vary in details. According to the Greek text,[6] the apostles are said to have been brought to Mary's side several days before her death—Peter from Rome, Paul from Tiberia (near Rome), Thomas from India, and so on. Those who had already died were "raised by the Holy Spirit out of their tombs," but instructed that this was not the resurrection for which all Christians wait. Each of the apostles described how they had been snatched up by a cloud of light and transported to Bethlehem to be with Mary. Even the sun and moon are said to have appeared near Mary's house, and these events brought many healings to those who gathered nearby: the blind received their sight, the deaf were given hearing, lepers were cleansed, and so on, just as we read in the Gospels concerning the ministry of Jesus. The story also features opposition to Mary from certain Jewish priests because they believed she had ruined the Jewish nation by bringing Jesus into the world.

Finally, on the day of Mary's death, Jesus himself appeared, along with an innumerable number of angels. The final exchanges between Mother and Son are described in this account, including her request that he "glorify those that glorify Thee through my name." He granted it. She then went to each of the apostles and blessed each one with her hand. Then Jesus stretched out his hands toward her and received her soul. The apostles buried her body in a new tomb in Gethsemane, and those who stayed near her tomb reported that they heard angels singing over the next three days. According to one version, when the singing stopped, they knew that her body had been taken to heaven; another version says that "twelve clouds of light snatched up the apostles, with the body of our Lady, and translated them to paradise."

This account of Mary's death and the transfer of her body into heaven has acquired great significance inasmuch as it provides the textual basis for the Catholic doctrine known as the Assumption of Mary, which was proclaimed in 1950 by Pope Pius XII. The traditional account of Mary's unique death is thought to be traceable to apostolic times, however, and is supported by the widespread early belief that no relics of her body existed and that the tomb where she had been placed was later found to be empty. The claim that Jesus and his apostles were all assembled at Mary's bedside when she died might strike those of a modern mindset as a fable, but a similar claim about an appearance of Jesus and his apostles was made in the twentieth century.

Gulshan Esther reports that Jesus and his apostles all appeared to her when she was a devout Muslim living in Pakistan with no knowledge of Christianity beyond the little information found in the Quran.[7] During this encounter, Gulshan was healed from her crippled condition and taught the Lord's Prayer. It was her knowledge of this prayer that convinced a Christian missionary in Pakistan to risk his right to stay in the country by catechizing her. Gulshan now lives in Oxford, England, and conducts frequent missions to Pakistan. She is well-known to friends of mine, who believe her story of the encounter. This case involves critical scrutiny in a way that the accounts involving the Virgin Mary do not, and the appearance of Jesus and his apostles offers supporting evidence for their appearance together at Mary's death.

More accounts of encounters with Jesus are included in the apocryphal books, but the ones mentioned above illustrate some of the allegations about such encounters that were made just after the Christian faith emerged.

Notes

[1] I do not want to go further into issues of language here—language should serve us, not coerce us into decisions about the nature of death, an issue that has become more complex due to modern medicine and its marvels.

[2] Willis Barnstone, ed., *The Other Bible* (San Francisco: Harper, 1984), xviii.

[3] This quote is from chapter 11 in the Ethiopic version.

[4] Wilhelm Schneemelcher, *New Testament Apocrypha*, vol. 1, rev. ed. (Cambridge: James Clarke, 1991), 1:348.

[5] Augustine, *The Literal Meaning of Genesis*, trans., J. H. Taylor (New York: Newman Press, 1982), 12.3.4.

[6] "The Book of John Concerning the Falling Asleep of Mary," in *The Writing of the Fathers Down to A.D. 325*, eds., A. Roberts and J. Donaldson (Grand Rapids, Mich.: Eerdmans, 1956), vol. 8.

[7] Esther, Gulshan, *The Torn Veil: The Story of Sister Gulshan Esther*, as told to Thelma Sangster (London: Marshall Pickering, 1992).

CHAPTER 2

VISIONS IN ANCIENT AND MEDIEVAL TIMES

No comprehensive account of the visions of Jesus reported in history has been attempted, to my knowledge, and I will not try to provide that here. The experience seems to have occurred frequently enough that finding all the accounts in various languages would be an impossible task.

Many accounts of visions of Jesus can be found in the biographies of people who have been recognized as saints in Roman Catholic faith, and I will try to give some sense here of the different kinds of experiences they reported. Other accounts come from people not officially designated as saints, and these accounts will be presented in approximate chronological order in order to show that visions of Jesus have been part of the ongoing life of the church.

No serious doubt seems to exist that visions of Jesus have occurred and might continue today. Even those who are skeptical about the reality of religious experiences seem to agree that such visions have occurred, although they tend to dismiss them as hallucinations in order to avoid giving them any value for religion. However, the lack of significant doubts about the occurrence of visions serves as silent testimony to the fact that enough reports have occurred in the history of the church to make such reports believable.

Common wisdom has it that only Christians have visions of Jesus and that only Catholics have visions of Mary. I question these generalizations because I do not think enough is known about exactly who has had such experiences in either the distant or the recent past. I will comment in a later chapter about the religious backgrounds of the thirty people who described their visionary experiences to me.

Accounts of Encounters

Some of the information that follows about the lives of various saints is drawn from the *Catholic Encyclopedia*. However, neither this encyclopaedia nor the *New Catholic Encyclopedia* describes in much detail the visions of the saints. We are more likely to find such information in what might be described as the "devotional literature" of the church, as opposed to its "academic literature." I am indebted for many of the accounts in this and the next chapter to the books authored by William J. Walsh and E. Cobham Brewer cited below. Brewer does not say much about his sources, while Walsh says he obtained some of his information from various periodicals, including *Ave Maria, Messenger of the Sacred Heart, Pilgrim of Our Lady of Martyrs, Rosary Magazine, Irish Monthly, Our Lady's Dowry,* and *Lives of the Saints*. However, Walsh does not specifically cite his sources in his accounts.

A curious example from the *Catholic Encyclopedia* is its entry on Saint Teresa of Avila. Although Teresa is widely known from her autobiography to have had various visions of Jesus, this article does not say much about them, only noting, "Meanwhile God had begun to visit her with 'intellectual visions and locutions,' that is *manifestations in which the exterior senses were in no way affected*, the things seen and the words heard being directly impressed upon her mind."[1] I have shown elsewhere that many of Teresa's recent interpreters have maintained that she had imaginative visions, not intellectual ones (following Augustine's threefold classification of visions).[2] I also argued there that Teresa provides grounds to think that she considered some of her visions to be corporeal, which would mean that her exterior senses *were* involved. However, she might not have wanted to admit to corporeal visions because the church considered such visions more likely to be diabolical than divine.

Many church officials—whether Protestant or Catholic—seem to be intent on minimizing the significance of visions or apparitions in Christian experience and, when obligated to acknowledge their existence, prefer to construe these encounters as intellectual (or perhaps imaginative) visions, not corporeal ones. Saint John of the Cross remarks in one place, for example, that Mary Magdalene's attempt to touch Jesus when she encountered him outside his tomb, as described in the New Testament, consisted of an inferior method of establishing his reality after his resurrection.

However, the original claim that Jesus was resurrected crucially depends upon sense experiences of those who encountered him after the resurrection; therefore, to minimize the value of sense experience is to undermine the ground upon which Christian faith rests. I can understand the Church's concern to encourage the faithful not to give undue significance to sense experience, but such mysterious experiences as visions and apparitions should not be misrepresented out of zeal for the well-being of the laity. I consider the skepticism about visions that is often exhibited by those with an "academic stance" to be excessive.

Saint Martha (First Century)

Martha, the sister of Mary and Lazarus according to the account in Saint John 11, is said to have seen Jesus during a visit he made to her home in France. According to oral tradition, Martha fled from Bethany along with her brother and sister and several other disciples when a persecution against Christians broke out in Palestine fourteen years after the death of Jesus. This little group of pilgrims crossed the Mediterranean and landed in France after their persecutors set them adrift in a small boat with neither sails nor oars. They came ashore in a port near Marseilles, where Lazarus remained to plant a church.

Martha traveled inland to Tarascon, where she introduced the Christian faith to that French community. She is reputed to have exorcised demons, healed the sick, and to have revived a man who drowned after falling into the Rhone River while listening to her sermon. Three bishops—Saint Maximin from Aix, Trophimus from Arles, and Eutropius from Orange—are said to have come to her house in order to consecrate it as a Christian church, but Martha apparently had no wine for her guests, so "Jesus Christ Himself came and changed some water into wine, which the bishops greatly commended."[3]

Brewer notes that the source of this account was Monsignor Guerin, chamberlain of Pope Leo XIII. Brewer then remarks: "A tale so full of anachronisms can scarcely be matched; but be it remembered that this biography is recorded in the nineteenth century as a history worthy of all men to be received and believed."[4] Though Brewer is seldom critical of either the stories he conveys or the sources for those stories, this one was evidently too much for him to believe, despite having a pope's chamberlain as an intermediary for its source.

An inescapable difficulty arising from accounts of events such as this one, which ordinarily would be said to be miraculous, is that many people today are skeptical about reports of miracles. This skepticism can be decried and denounced by people in the Church, but it remains a significant feature of our age. However, I am convinced that Aristotle was on the right track when he replied to an objection to the idea that some people could prophesy the future in their dreams about upcoming events. He said that we should be neither too skeptical nor too gullible about such claims. Such an attitude is particularly appropriate when we confront allegations about a particular kind of experience, such as a vision of Jesus, that has evidently occurred many times. Whereas any single account might be unbelievable, I think that too many reports of such visions have been given to reject them all. However, this cautious attitude toward reports of extraordinary events does not solve the problem in the case of a particular allegation, such as this one about Martha and the bishops. I can understand Brewer's hesitation to accept the report at face value.

Pope Alexander I (Second Century)

Various people report seeing Jesus as an infant or a little child, including Pope Alexander I in the year 118. Saint Irenaeus of Lyons, writing late in the second century, identifies Alexander as the fifth pope in succession from the first apostles.[5] Alexander is said to have introduced the use of blessing water mixed with salt for the purification of Christian homes from evil influences. According to a tradition found in the Roman Church, he suffered a martyr's death by decapitation.

Important questions remain about how those who see Jesus as an infant or a child are able to recognize him. Sometimes Jesus is seen in the arms of his mother, and sometimes other heavenly visitors interact with the visionary and so identify the person who is encountered. Moreover, an extraordinary kind of knowledge is often ascribed to those who have remarkable experiences involving spiritual realities.

Saint Peter of Alexandria (Fourth Century)

Peter lived in the age of Diocletian, who ruled the eastern portion of the Roman empire, when Galerius was Caesar.[6] In 303 Diocletian introduced a persecution of the Christian church, with the encouragement of Galerius, and another group of Christians were martyred. As Peter was preaching one day, the soldiers of Diocletian entered the church and seized him, intending to take him to Nicomedia. The people opposed the soldiers with such persuasion that Peter was imprisoned beside the church.

As Patriarch of Alexandria, Peter had excommunicated Arius (250–336), who denied the divinity of Jesus and taught that he was only a superior creation. When Peter was in prison, a number of priests and deacons that supported the Arian heresy visited him to ask that Arius might be forgiven and reinstated. Because of their persistence, he divulged to several of his faithful priests an event that had taken place when he was only twelve years old. Peter explained that when he was in prayer one day, Jesus had appeared to him, his face full of light and brilliantly aglow. His robe, however, had been torn in two, and he was trying to hold it together so that his nakedness would not be seen. Peter asked him who had torn his robe, and Jesus replied: "Arius hath rent it, and by all means beware of receiving him into communion . . . lay thy commands upon Achillas and Alexander the priests, who after thy translation will rule my Church, not by any means to receive him."

Shortly after his imprisonment, Peter made arrangements with the Roman tribune who guarded him to leave his prison secretly so that the people who supported him would not put up a fight to prevent his execution. At midnight, as November 24, 311, was dawning, he gave himself to his executioners, and went to the place where the apostle Mark had been martyred. There he knelt and entreated Saint Mark to be made worthy of martyrdom, and submitted himself to beheading. A few days later, the persecutions stopped, as Constantine the Great became emperor.

The Catholic Encyclopedia identifies the account of this vision of Jesus as coming from the Acts of the Martyrdom of Saint Peter, and says that they are too late to have any historical value.[7]

Saint Catherine of Alexandria, Egypt (Fourth Century)

Catherine was born of noble parents and was intellectually gifted.[8] She studied the doctrines of Christianity out of curiosity but refrained from submitting her mind to the faith. She is said to have had a vision of Mary holding Jesus in her arms, but when Catherine went to caress him, he turned away. She embraced Christian faith because of this experience, and shortly afterward had another vision of the Virgin and Child, who then pressed her to his heart and placed a ring on her finger.

Catherine presented herself to the Roman emperor Maximin at only eighteen years of age to protest the persecution of Christians.[9] She was then forced to debate various scholars, some of whom were converted by her arguments and were immediately executed. She too was finally beheaded, but not before having been a significant influence. Her body is said to have been miraculously taken by angels to Mount Sinai, where a monastery and church were built in her honor. The author of the article in *The Catholic Encyclopedia* also remarks that many of the stories associated with her are, in his opinion, legends.

Saint Jerome (Fourth Century)

Jerome (Eusebius Hieronymus Sophronius) was born in Stridon, Italy, in about 347 to an affluent Christian family, who sent him to Rome to be educated.[10] When he was about twenty, he was baptized and became interested in ecclesiastical matters. From Rome he went to Trier, famous for its schools, and there began his theological studies. He settled first in Antioch, and for some years led an austere life in the desert of Chalcis, southwest of Antioch. Jerome was known for his outspokenness, and his harsh criticisms made him some bitter enemies. In 386 he settled in a monastery in Bethlehem near a convent founded by two Roman women, Paula and Eustochium, who followed him to Palestine, where he died in 420. He is known for a life of asceticism and study, which was also marked by controversies.

Jerome describes a divine encounter in 374 in which he was beaten for his love of Cicero and his neglect of the Scriptures. This event happened after Jerome suffered from a fever that almost took his life. He writes:

> Suddenly I was caught up in the spirit and dragged before the judgment seat of the Judge; and here the light was so bright, and those who stood around were so radiant, that I cast myself upon the ground and did not dare to look up. Asked who and what I was I replied: "I am a Christian." But He who presided said: "Thou liest, thou art a follower of Cicero and not of Christ."[11]

At this point, Christ ordered Jerome to be scourged, until he began to beg for mercy. His punishment stopped when he swore that he would neither possess nor read the worldly books of which he was so fond. He continues:

Dismissed, then, on taking this oath, I returned to the upper world, and, to the surprise of all, I opened upon them eyes so drenched with tears that my distress served to convince even the incredulous. And that this was no sleep nor idle dream, such as those by which we are often mocked, I call to witness the tribunal before which I lay, and the terrible judgment which I feared. May it never, hereafter, be my lot to fall under such an inquisition! I profess that my shoulders were black and blue, that I felt the bruises long after I awoke from my sleep, and that thenceforth I read the books of God.[12]

This story is interesting because it reports effects that might be seen by any observer, even if the visionary experience involved scenes that others could not see. Jerome clearly mentions flagellation in order to defend the objectivity of the experience. However, various authors who have commented on the experience consider it to have been a dream. In a later chapter, I will describe the twentieth-century experience of Jim Link, who said he was interrogated by Christ for leading a lackluster Christian life. An observable feature of his experience was reported by his brother-in-law and the wives of Jim and his brother-in-law, who could not get near Jim during the time he said he was being interrogated—as though an invisible zone had been created that they could not penetrate for several hours. The objectivity of ancient experiences is easy to question, but the dynamics are different when we meet people living today who report similar "encounters."

Saint Philomena of Rome, and Saints Julian and Basilissa of Egypt (Fourth Century)

Philomena, born of noble parents at Nicopolis in Macedonia, is said to have been tortured and executed for her faith under the Roman emperor Diocletian. Three days before her execution she was visited by the Blessed Virgin, who placed the child Jesus in her arms.[13] Walsh remarks that the history of her martyrdom "is not based on romantic imagination, but on private revelations made by the saint in 1836 to three different people."[14] The article on Philomena in *The Catholic Encyclopedia* expresses doubt that someone of her name was martyred. The author of the article was evidently unimpressed with the information about Philomena that came from visionaries who lived about 1,500 years after she died.

Other martyrs from this same century are also reported to have seen Jesus and his Mother. Julian and Basilissa, who were husband and wife but lived by mutual consent in chastity, underwent persecution for their faith, and finally were martyred by Maximin.[15] On the day of their martyrdom, Jesus and Mary are said to have appeared to them, surrounded by saints and angels.

Saint Barbara (Fourth Century)

Barbara was born in Nicomedia (Izmit) in Asia in 306 during the reign of Maximus.[16] Accounts vary of the events that led to her execution, and some critics regard all of these accounts as legendary. Her father, Dioscorus, was a ruler who kept his daughter a virgin by locking her up in a tower whenever he was away. He came home one day and discovered she was following the Christian faith and so had her tortured and finally executed. Some say Jesus appeared to Barbara in prison and healed her, after her father had beaten and imprisoned her.[17] Another version of the story says that immediately following her execution, which Dioscorus is said to have performed by decapitation, he was struck dead by lightning, which might explain why Saint Barbara is often invoked during thunderstorms.

Some versions say the execution took place in her home city, and others say that Heliopolis in Egypt was the place she was killed. The execution has also been located in Nicomedia, Antioch, and Rome. The historical reliability of the events surrounding the life of Barbara is in question, for an early list of martyrs does not include her, which also casts doubt on the claim that Jesus appeared to and healed her in prison. Nonetheless, Barbara has been popular in the East and West since the seventh century.

Saint Porphyry (or Porphyrius) (Fourth or Fifth Century)

Porphyry was born at Thessalonica in about 347 and later became a bishop of Gaza in Palestine, where he died in 420.[18] He lived in an Egyptian desert for five years and then in a cave near the Jordan for five years. He often left that cave to visit the site of the resurrection in Jerusalem.

His health was poor, and on one occasion while in extreme pain, he was granted a vision in which he saw Jesus upon the cross along with the penitent thief.[19] He writes:

> About forty days ago when I was keeping the vigil of the holy day of the Lord, an unspeakable pain of the liver got hold upon me, and being unable to endure the anguish I went and lay down near the sacred Skull, and by reason of the great pain I fell as it were into a trance. And I see the Saviour nailed upon the Cross and one of the thieves with him hanging upon another cross, and I begin to cry out and speak the words of the thief, "Lord, remember me when thou comest into thy kingdom" [Luke 23: 42]. And the Saviour answereth and saith to the thief that is hanging "Go down from the cross and save him that is lying there, even as thou wast saved." And the thief came down from the cross and took me in his arms and kissed me, and stretching forth his

right hand raised me up, saying, "Come to the Saviour." And straightway I rose up and ran to him, and I see him coming down from the Cross and saying to me, "Take this wood and keep it." And I took the same precious wood and lifted it up, and straightway I came to myself out of my trance, and from that same hour there was no more pain in me, neither is the place of the disease manifest.[20]

The fact that Porphyry seems to have gone in and out of consciousness might suggest that the experience was a dream. However, in view of the fact that his pain is said to have disappeared, we could question whether the experience was merely a dream. If the familiar world is somehow altered because of an experience that some dismiss as purely subjective, we have grounds for believing that some form of objective reality—perhaps a supernatural form—is involved.

Experiences in which visionaries somehow see the sufferings of Christ are still reported today. In a study in the 1990s of people who mysteriously display stigmata, Ted Harrison reports that a twentieth-century stigmatic saw, among other things, "Christ being whipped, mocked and given the crown of thorns."[21] He does not supply more detail, however.

The widely respected, conservative Christian magazine *Christianity Today* recently reported that a collective appearance of a suffering Jesus was witnessed in China. The account comes from Karen Feaver, a legislative assistant for U.S. Congressman Frank Wolf of Virginia. She reports that as a Christian message was preached to a crowd unfamiliar with Christianity, "a vision of Jesus walking among them and then suffering on the cross appeared to all gathered. When the teacher told of Jesus rising from the dead, the vision showed Jesus ascending to heaven gloriously."[22] These experiences are reminiscent of what is reported of Saint Veronica of Milan, who was shown the life of Jesus in a series of visions in the fifteenth century.[23]

It is difficult to understanding how people could experience what seem to be visual re-enactments of past events "not as a dream but as real life," which is how H. A. Baker describes this experience.[24] A collective experience belongs in a different category of evidence than a private one. When several people report seeing the same thing simultaneously, the matter they report is apparently real, although the spiritual realities encountered are such that we probably should be cautious about insisting that what is seen exists exactly the way it appears.

Other significant collective encounters of Jesus come to us from early Christian history. For example, Brewer reports that an event occurred in the year 320 when Jesus visited forty Christian soldiers in prison prior to their execution—they had refused to offer sacrifices to pagan deities.[25] Such an encounter with the living Christ, which resembles the collective experiences we have with ordinary objects in everyday life, provides strong grounds for thinking they had an encounter with a real being. I consider the term *vision* to be inappropriate to describe such experiences, although I think that there are few standards for correctly using this term so would not fault anyone who did describe them as visions. Some people might prefer the term *apparition*, and the term *appearance* also seems suitable.

To me, the report of the experience of the forty Christian soldiers in 320 seems somehow less believable than does the recent report of the collective experience in China. I cannot account for these "instinctive responses" to the two accounts, and I am prepared to consider the possibility that I am unreasonably suspicious of very old reports. I surmise that my responses are shaped by the thought that an educated person living today, which Karen Feaver is, recognizes she has a lot to lose by advancing an implausible account of an extraordinary religious event in a cultural climate that is often highly critical of religion. By contrast, Brewer does not say anything about the source of his story of the forty Christian soldiers, and I suspect that people might have been more easily able to get away with false reports of extraordinary religious events from 1,700 years ago. However, my assumption could be mistaken.

Saint Honore (Honorius) (Sixth Century)

Saint Honore was a Roman monk, who either accompanied Saint Augustine (not the famous Saint Augustine of Hippo) to Britain in 596 or was one of the second group of missionaries sent to Britain in 601.[26] Honore is known for having been effective in converting the inhabitants of Kent, and he was elected Archbishop of Canterbury in 627, the fifth after Saint Augustine. A letter to him from the pope shows that his life was spent in fulfilling the duties of his office and in the faithful observance of the rule of his master, Saint Gregory. He died in about 653.

Saint Honore reported that Jesus once came to him and administered the holy elements to him with his own hands.[27] He is not the only person who reported seeing the Mass celebrated by Jesus Christ. Emperor Saint Henry reported that he saw Jesus enter Saint Mary Major's church in Rome in 1014 to celebrate Mass, accompanied by many saints and angels. One of the angels came up to Henry and touched his thigh, whereupon he became lame and remained so for the rest of his life.[28]

Gregory the Great and Peter the Banker (Sixth Century)

A number of ancient accounts describe saints giving gifts to the poor and then being surprised to find that Jesus was the recipient. One of the earliest such accounts is that of Saint Gregory the Great

(540–604), who regularly gave to beggars. One night after Gregory had fed the poor, Jesus appeared to him and said, "Ordinarily you receive me in the poor that assemble at your board, but today you received Me personally."[29] Gregory also tells an interesting story about caring for the poor, in which Jesus appeared in 494 to a priest of Mount Preclaro who was about to sit down to dinner. Jesus instructed the monk to bring food to Saint Benedict, saying, "Thou hast provided good cheer for thyself, and my servant in such a place is afflicted with hunger."[30]

Some years later a banker named Peter is said to have encountered Jesus in the form of a beggar. In 619 Peter had a dream in which his shortcomings were revealed, and as a result, gave away most of his wealth, even giving his coat to a beggar. However, Peter was annoyed when the beggar turned around and sold the coat to someone else. On his way home that day, Peter met Jesus wearing his coat; he commended Peter for his generosity and then disappeared. Peter responded by giving away all his possessions.[31]

Ss. Wulsin (Tenth Century) and Raymund Nonnatus (Thirteenth Century)

Saint Wulsin, bishop of Sherbourne in Dorsetshire, as he lay dying in 983, is said to have seen Jesus at the right hand of God.[32] I have been unable to find out more about this reported experience, but it bears resemblance to that of Saint Stephen whose martyrdom is described by Luke in Acts of the Apostles. Saint Raymund Nonnatus of Catalonia is also said to have had a deathbed vision of Jesus, who anointed him, in 1240. The source of this report is the *Annals of the Order of Our Lady of Mercy*, to which Raymund belonged.[33]

Conrad, Bishop of Constance (Tenth Century)

Einsiedeln, Switzerland, was the location of a hermitage where a monk was murdered in 853. For the next fifty years the hermitage had no tenant, until it was restored by some Benedictines in 906. In 948 Conrad, bishop of Constance, went to consecrate a monastery and church on the site.[34] The night before the consecration, the bishop went to the church to pray. At midnight a light more brilliant than the sun illuminated the sanctuary, and he heard the sound of melodious voices. Looking up, the bishop saw two choirs of angels, and the Lord himself standing at the high altar, arrayed in pontifical vestments and preparing to celebrate the Mass of dedication. He was assisted by Saints Stephen, Lawrence, Peter, Gregory, and Augustine. Before the altar was the Virgin Mother, seated on a throne of light, attended by angels. The startled bishop observed the Mass celebrated by the heavenly court, and was still kneeling in an ecstatic trance when the sun came up and people filled the church for the dedication. The bishop was not aware that the service was about to begin, and he was finally asked to take his place. He informed those who were to assist him that the church had already been divinely consecrated, and then described the vision he had seen. When he was about to utter the first words of the service of consecration, a voice was distinctly heard to say, "Cease, brother! For the church has been divinely consecrated."

Robert of Lyons (Twelfth Century)

Robert of Lyons was shown the heavenly city in a vision in 1109, after he had asked God to show him the path to heaven.[35] He found himself separated from the city by a river, and on the opposite bank were around a dozen poor men washing their clothes. Among them was one who had a robe of dazzling whiteness, helping the others. This dazzling figure said to Robert, "I am Jesus Christ, ever ready to help the truly penitent."[36]

Saint William of Vercelli (or of Monte Vergine, Italy) (Twelfth Century)

William is best known for having founded the Hermits of Monte Vergine, also known as the Williamites.[37] He was born to nobility in 1084 and educated by a relative when both of his parents died. At age fifteen he made up his mind to renounce the world and lead a life of penance. So he went on a taxing pilgrimage, encircling his body with iron bands to increase his suffering. He built himself a hut on Monte Vergine, wishing to become a hermit and live in solitude, but many people flocked to him, being attracted by the sanctity of his life and the many miracles he performed. In 1119 he established the Congregation of Monte Vergine and stayed until his fellow monks objected to him, saying that the life he advocated was too austere, and that he gave too much in alms. He went on to establish other monasteries.

Soon after his arrival at Mount Vergine, the Virgin appeared to him, holding in her arms the divine Infant, who made known to William that he was to build a Christian temple on the spot, which once had been a temple of Cybele.[38] He died in 1142 at the monastery he had established at Gugieto.

Blessed Hermann Joseph, of Cologne, Germany (Twelfth Century)

Hermann was born the son of poor parents in 1150 and at a young age began his devotion to the Virgin Mary that he would be known for his whole life. At every available moment he could be found at the church of Saint Mary,[39] kneeling in prayer. He is said to have once presented an apple to Jesus, saved from his own scarce meal, who apparently accepted it. According to another legend, Mary supplied him with shoes.[40]

As a child, Hermann reported that he saw the Virgin Mary floating in the air above him as he approached the altar of the church he would visit on his way to school.[41] She was accompanied by Saint John, who was playing with the infant Jesus. Mary invited Hermann to join them, and he was raised into the air, where he stayed for a while until Mary took him down to the floor. He reported that events of this kind were often repeated. Hermann entered a Premonstratensian monastery when he was twelve and lived there until his death in 1241 at about 90 years old.

Hermann's claim of Jesus as a playmate is reminiscent of Anne Catherine Emmerich, the child of poor parents living in Flamske, Germany, in the eighteenth century, who is said to have had Mary and Jesus as constant companions as a child.

Saint Francis of Assisi (Thirteenth Century)

Francis is well-known, primarily because of the large monastic order he founded and because of his fame for sanctity and a life of discipline and service of the poor. He was born in Assisi in Umbria in 1181 or 1182 and died there in 1226. His father was a wealthy merchant, but Francis felt compelled to give away what he had and embrace a life of poverty.

Once, when Francis was praying before an ancient crucifix in the out-of-the-way chapel of Saint Damian's below Assisi, he heard a voice that said, "Go, Francis, and repair my house, which as you see is falling into ruin." He first took this literally but was rebuffed by the priest. Later he interpreted it as a call to rebuild the church through the Franciscan Order. These monks worked with the laborers in the fields, and when no one gave them work they would beg. In a short while, Francis and his companions gained an immense influence, and men of different walks in life and ways of thought flocked to the order. He also established the first monastery of the Second Franciscan Order of Poor Ladies, now known as Poor Clares.

Francis's life and ministry featured many miracles, among which the appearance of stigmata are the most famous. It was on or about September 14, 1224, while Francis was praying on the mountainside, that he saw a vision of an angel. After that, the visible marks of the five wounds of Jesus crucified appeared on his body. Francis's right side was described as bearing an open wound that looked as if it had been made by a lance, while through his hands and feet were black nails of flesh with the points bent backward. After the reception of the stigmata, Francis suffered increasing pains throughout his already frail body.

In 1221 Francis saw Jesus, Jesus' mother, and a multitude of angels; two years later Jesus appeared again to him, this time giving him three white and three red roses "as an external ratification of the reality of his vision, it being in the midst of winter, when a rose was nowhere to be found."[42]

Princess Ermesinde (Thirteenth Century)

In 1214 Princess Ermesinde of Clairefontaine, Luxembourg, while asleep, saw the heavens open "and a Lady of enchanting beauty lightly descending on a fleecy cloud."[43] In her hands this lady held an infant of unsurpassed beauty, with whom she approached the Princess, who was sitting at the fountain of Saint Bernard. The woman and baby stopped as they reached the fountain. The Princess was then shown some white lambs, on each of which were black bands that formed a cross. Then she awoke and resolved to build a convent near that spot.

The remarkable feature of this "dream" is that the Princess envisioned events that corresponded to the place where she was, for she was actually at the fountain of Saint Bernard, which he blessed when he visited it seven centuries earlier. In the dream the events were "seen" at that exact locale. Supposed dreams that feature the places where the dreamers are actually located are extraordinary and suggest that something more is being communicated than what is usually found in ordinary dreams. One such dream is described in Genesis 15, in which Abraham cut up animals in preparation for a sacrifice, fell into a deep sleep, and then "saw" the Lord himself walk between the pieces that lay beside Abraham.

Saint Rose of Viterbo (Thirteenth Century)

Saint Rose was born at Viterbo in 1235 to poor and pious parents, and she died before her eighteenth birthday.[44] When she was only twelve, she preached about penance to the citizens of Viterbo and attracted such an admiring following that the envious prefect of the city decided to banish her. She went to Vitorchiano and converted many citizens, including a sorceress, by standing unscathed for three hours in the flames of a burning pyre. But she was denied entry into the monastery of Saint Mary of the Roses and spent the rest of her life in a cell in her father's house, where she died.

Rose once saw Jesus suspended on his cross, nailed by his hands and feet, and crowned with thorns. His body bore many marks of torture and abuse, and she fainted at the sight of it. When she recovered consciousness, she is said to have gazed at him and conversed with him, in which conversation he told her of his love for the whole human race.[45]

Saint Agnes of Monte Pulciano (Thirteenth Century)

Saint Agnes was born in Tuscany in 1268 and entered a convent at a very young age.[46] After a few years she was sent to assist in the founding of another convent in Porcena, where she became the abbess when she was only fifteen. She is said to have been favored with frequent visions, and on ten occasions received communion from an angel's hand. After seventeen years at Porcena, the inhabitants of Monte Pulciano urged her to establish a convent there. As she prayed about this request, she saw a vision in which three well-equipped boats floated before her. In one of the boats stood Saint Augustine; in another was Saint Francis; and in the third stood Saint Dominic. Each wished her to step aboard, as though they were competing for her allegiance. She stepped onto Saint Dominic's boat in the vision, signifying that the women who followed Saint Agnes to Monte Pulciano were to follow the rule of Saint Dominic.

One day when Agnes was in Porcena, the Virgin Mary appeared to her and placed the Infant Jesus in her arms. Before she returned the child to its mother, Agnes took a little cross from him that was suspended from his neck by a slender thread. She somehow left this cross behind when she left Porcena to go to Mount Pulciano, and when she wrote and asked the community at Porcena to send her the cross, they refused. At this point, Walsh says, "Whereupon the Saint betook herself to prayer, and it was immediately brought to her by an angel."[47]

The claim that the cross—an object presumably having its origin in the invisible world—was taken from the Infant Jesus perhaps strains the credulity of someone of the modern age, but no more so than the claim that Saint Agnes was given communion by angels. In my interviews with people who reported that Jesus had appeared to them, a woman told me she had been given communion by Christ himself. She said that she was taken to a place where she met her deceased parents and then met the Lord. She spoke of having embraced Jesus and of having the unique tactile sensation of touching the clothes he wore, which seemed to her to be made of linen. Modern experiences shed light on claims such as the one made about Saint Agnes, which is nearly 800 years old.

Saints Gertrude and Mechtilde of Heldelfs, Germany (Thirteenth Century)

Gertrude was born to a countess in 1263; by her fifth birthday she had been placed in a Benedictine convent where she was soon joined by her younger sister, Mechtilde (see below).[48] Gertrude experienced locutions in which Mary and her Son communicated insights regarding spiritual life. In 1294 Gertrude was chosen abbess, and her community moved to Heldelfs. She served in this capacity for forty years. Soon after she assumed her office, Jesus appeared to her, bearing a magnificent building on his shoulders. He said to her:

> Behold with what labor, care, and vigilance I carry this beloved house, which is none other than that of religion. It is everywhere threatened with ruin, because there are so few persons who are willing to do or to suffer anything for its support and increase. You, therefore, should suffer with me in bearing it; for all those who endeavor, by their words or actions, to extend religion, and who try to re-establish it in its first fervor and purity, are so many pillars which sustain this holy house; and comfort me by sharing with me the weight of this burden.[49]

Near the end of her life Gertrude lost her ability to speak and suffered other ailments. A month before her death, the Lord appeared to her in the form of a spouse, extended his arms toward her, and invited her to himself. When the day of her death came, Jesus again appeared to her in joy and radiance; his mother was at his right hand, and the beloved disciple John was at his left. A large band of virgins also are said to have appeared to the members of the convent.

Mechtilde was born in 1264, and at the age of seven was placed in the Benedictine convent where her sister also lived. She soon became a model of virtue, and taught her convent sisters to follow her example. Before long she became a superioress, and belonged to several convents, including one in Diessen in Bavaria. She experienced many visions and locutions and described some of these for posterity. She once had a vision on the Feast of the Assumption, which she was unable to celebrate fully because she was sick. As she fervently prayed, the Holy Mother appeared to her in glory, clothed in a green mantle covered with golden flowers enriched with precious stones.

Seeing this, Mechtilde besought Jesus to obtain Mary's favor for her, because Mechtilde felt that she had not been sufficiently devoted to her. Jesus then expressed his affection for his mother, and Mary in turn expressed her affection for Mechtilde. The service to celebrate the Feast was progressing as this was happening, and when the prayers for the day began, Jesus renewed in Mary the joys she had experienced when he was conceived and then born. As prayers continued, Mechtilde then saw Mary spread out her mantle to protect all those who come to her for refuge.

On one occasion Mechtilde was shown a vision of Jesus seated on a high throne, around which her sister Gertrude walked without turning her eyes from him even for a moment.[50] He then commended Gertrude for the care and fidelity with which she fulfilled her duties.

This experience of being able to walk around a visionary object would give the objects in the vision a sense of reality, inasmuch as not only the visual sense is involved in such an experience, but the kinesthetic sense that provides us with knowledge of where we are in space and how other objects are oriented in relation to us.

Blessed Benvenuta Bojani (Thirteenth Century)

Benvenuta was born in Austria, the seventh daughter in a family wishing for a son.[51] Her name means *welcome* in Italian, signifying her father's decision to welcome her into the family. She exhibited remarkable piety from an early age and soon learned to add fasting and other disciplines to her regimen of prayer. The extreme acts of self-denial and penitence, which were secretly performed, damaged her health, but Saint Dominic appeared to her, instructing her to disclose all her actions to her confessor. He compelled her to exercise moderation. During this period, she struggled with forces that tempted her with evil, and for five years she became so sick she could not keep her food down. After a pilgrimage to the tomb of Saint Dominic, Benvenuta's health was restored.

One day when she was in prayer she saw a beautiful child and asked him if he was able to say the Hail Mary prayer. He replied, "Can you say it?" Benvenuta immediately began the recitation. When she came to the words, "Blessed is the fruit of your womb," the child said, "And I am he," and disappeared.

Another time, as she prayed that Mary might allow her to see the Child Jesus, she was shown a lady bearing an infant in her arms, accompanied by an old man. The lady instructed Benvenuta to return home, promising that she would there see what she desired. When Benvenuta reached her home she saw the same vision. Mary is said to have laid the Holy Child in her arms and allowed her to caress the child for more than an hour.

This experience of holding the Holy Child was also reported by Saint Walthen (also spelled 'Waltheof') of Scotland, a descendant of William the Conqueror. Walthen once lifted the sacred host (communion wafer) and pronounced the words of consecration; suddenly, the host disappeared and in his arms lay a lovely babe, smiling and stretching its arms to caress him. Suddenly the child disappeared, and the sacred host lay on the altar.[52]

Blessed Angela (Fourteenth Century)

Angela was born at Foligno in Umbria in 1248, to a rich family.[53] She was married at an early age but loved the world and its pleasures and so fell into sin and a disorderly life. She eventually was converted and told the story of her early life in "Book of Visions and Instructions." Eventually, Angela joined the Third Order of Saint Francis and became known for her holiness. She established a community of sisters at Foligno and died in 1309.

Angela once saw Jesus sitting by the side of his mother. This vision, which she says lasted for three days, allowed her to understand the depth of his sufferings and humiliations. On several other occasions she was given the Infant Jesus to hold by his Mother. Angela is also said to have seen Jesus at her death in 1309, when he showed her the royal robe of light with which a soul is clothed at death. Exactly how Jesus showed her this robe is not explained, and further probing of such questions might yield few answers. Strange events continue to be reported in close association with death. Both my father and my mother-in-law report seeing great joy and radiance come over their fathers just as they died, which many interpret as either seeing Jesus or angels.

Saint Alexis Falconieri (Fourteenth century)

Alexis was born near Florence in the year 1200, the son of a merchant prince, who was also one of the leaders of the Republic.[54] Alexis joined the Laudesi, a pious confraternity of the Blessed Virgin, and there met the six future companions of his life of holiness. In 1233 he and his six companions experienced an apparition of Mary. The seven soon afterward founded the Order of the Servites. So deep and sincere was Alexis's humility that, though he lived to the great age of 110 years, he always refused to enter the priesthood, of which he deemed himself unworthy. He confined his duties primarily to the material needs of the various communities in which he lived.

At his death, he was visited by the Infant Jesus in visible form, according to eyewitnesses. Knowing his hour of death was at hand, Alexis called his brothers to be with him and recited 100 Ave Marias. As he recited the last one, he saw Jesus approach and crown him with fragrant flowers. He cried out: "Kneel my brothers, see ye not Jesus Christ, your loving Lord and mine, who crowns me with a garland of beauteous flowers? Worship Him and adore. He will crown you also in the same manner, if, full of devotion to the holy Virgin, you imitate her immaculate purity, her profound humility."[55]

Saint Bridget of Sweden (Fourteenth Century)

Bridget was born about 1303, the daughter of Birger Persson, governor and provincial judge of Uppland, and Ingeborg, both of royal descent. [56] At the hour of her birth, a priest is said to have seen above her parents' house a brilliant cloud in the midst of which sat a woman holding a book.[57] At the age of thirteen, she was married to a noble and pious husband, and their union was blessed with eight children. The saintly life and the great charity of Bridget made her famous, and she later joined the court of King Magnus Eriksson, over whom she gradually acquired great influence. After the death of her husband in 1344, Bridget devoted herself entirely to religion. Her visions, which she said had begun in childhood, became more frequent and definite at this time of her life. She wrote down her revelations, which were widely respected during the Middle Ages.

Bridget was visited early in life by the Holy Mother, and when she was ten years old, Jesus appeared to her. He showed her how he appeared at his crucifixion and said to her, "See how I am maltreated. Look at me, my daughter." She asked who had done this to him, and he replied, "Those who despise me, and who are insensible to the love

I bear them." From that day on, Bridget was absorbed in contemplation of his sufferings.

Jesus revealed himself to her on another occasion, concerning
the death of her son Charles, who was a soldier. Bridget was trou-
bled about his salvation, for as a soldier he lived a dangerous life.
Mary revealed to Bridget that her son had found salvation, and then
she saw Jesus on his throne and the devil, who brought two accusa-
tions against Mary. The first was that Mary had hindered the devil
in tempting Charles at the hour of his death, and the second was that
Mary had presented the soul of Charles to judgment, and thus had
saved him without allowing the devil to bring charges against him.
Bridget then saw "the Judge banish Satan, and the soul of Charles
was carried to heaven."[58]

Bridget moved to Rome in 1349, where she lived until her death
in 1391.

Saint Catharine of Siena (Fourteenth Century)

Catharine was born in Siena, near Florence, in 1347, the youngest of
twenty-five children.[59] Her father was a dyer, and her mother was the
daughter of a poet. Her parents were known for their piety, and little
Catharine became known for hers at an early age. Her first vision
is said to have occurred when she was about six, while returning
home with her little brother Stephen from a visit to a married sister.[60]
As they passed the church of Saint Dominic, she saw a magnificent
throne above it, on which Jesus Christ was seated, wearing pontifical
robes and a tiara. Near him were Saints Peter, Paul, and John. As
Catharine gazed at Jesus, transfixed on the heavenly sight, he smiled
at her and made the sign of the cross over her. A few moments later,
her brother disturbed her reverie, wondering why she had lagged
behind. She looked at him, and then looked back to the place where

the vision had appeared, but by then it had disappeared. This was only the first of many visitations she is said to have experienced.

Catharine was known for the disciplines she practiced. She spent long hours night and day in prayer, abstained from meat and wine, and clothed herself in a rough hair shirt, or in iron chains that sank into her flesh. She sought in this way to expiate the sins of others. These disciplines left her weak and sick, but her ardor impressed the Order of Saint Dominic, which admitted her in spite of her young age. A life of prayer, contemplation, and mortification followed, as well as battles against temptation and dark forces that sought her undoing. Jesus appeared to her hanging on the Cross after a particularly terrible period of temptation, consoling her with the thought that he was with her in her trials.

Catharine is also said to have experienced espousal to Christ. He appeared to her, accompanied by the Virgin Mary, Saints John, Paul, and Dominic, and by King David, who played his harp. Mary advanced toward Catharine, took her by the hand, led her to Jesus and asked him to espouse Catharine to himself. Walsh describes the scene: "He consented by bowing His head, and taking out a ring set with four precious pearls with a marvelously rich diamond in the centre, put it on the finger of her right hand, saying these words: 'Behold I hereby espouse thee to Myself in faith.'" When the vision was finished, the ring is said to have stayed on her finger, although visible only to Catharine. She was graced with other encounters, including several in which Jesus appeared as a beggar and asked for alms. On both occasions he came to her the following night and commended her for her love.

Some people seem to be favored with many encounters during their lives, not only a single event. The reasons why particular individuals are singled out in this way are not clear.

Saint Vincent Ferrier (Fourteenth Century)

Vincent was born in 1350 at Valencia, the son of a man knighted for valor in the conquest of Valencia in 1238. Vincent completed his education in philosophy at the age of fourteen, and in 1367 he entered the Dominican Order. He was sent to study in Barcelona the following year, and during his stay there he once foretold the near approach of ships bearing wheat. His prediction was fulfilled. For twenty years he traversed western Europe, preaching penance for sin and preparation for judgment.

In 1398 he suffered an attack of fever that brought him near death, but during an apparition of Christ, who was accompanied by Saints Dominic and Francis, he was miraculously cured and sent to preach penance and prepare men for the coming judgment. In this experience, Jesus touched Vincent's face with his right hand, according to a letter Saint Vincent wrote to Pope Benedict XIII in 1411.[61] His following came from all over western Europe, including Genoa, Flanders, and Northern France. Since Vincent could speak only Limousin, the language of his native Valencia, many of his biographers believe that he was endowed with the gift of tongues, which is an opinion supported by Nicholas Clemangis, a doctor of the University of Paris, who had heard him preach.[62] Saint Vincent was also given divine graces that allowed him to work miracles of healing. He died in 1419.

Blessed Mary Mancini (Fourteenth Century)

Mary is said to have begun experiencing divine favors at the age of five. She was first married at age twelve years, and when her first husband passed away when she was sixteen, she married again. By twenty-four she was again a widow and resisted pressure from her family to marry a third time. Instead, she gave herself to a life of contemplation, austerity, and charity. One day she was visited by a young man, poorly clad and covered with wounds. She brought him to her house and dressed his sores. Before he left he laid his hand on her head and blessed her. After he departed, she drank some of the water used to wash his wounds, as a form of mortification, and found that it was unusually sweet. She wondered if she had been the recipient of a divine visitation, and was told by her guardian angel that Jesus himself had come to visit, in the form of a beggar.[63]

The medieval age was marked by beliefs in spiritual realities and beings that the modern era has found difficult, even impossible, to accept at face value. However, visions of Jesus continue to be reported.

Notes

[1] *Catholic Encyclopedia,* s.v. "St Teresa of Avila" (emphasis mine), ed. Charles Herbermann et. al. (New York: Robert Appleton, 1912).

[2] Phillip H. Wiebe, "The Christic Visions of Teresa of Avila," *Scottish Journal of Religion* 20 (1999), 73–86.

[3] E. Cobham Brewer, *A Dictionary of Miracles* (London: Chatto & Windus, 1884), 482.

[4] Brewer, *Dictionary,* 483.

[5] *Catholic Encyclopedia* s.v. "Pope Alexander I."

[6] Anastaius the Librarian, *Life of St. Peter of Alexandria,* The Saint Pachomius Orthodox Library, http://www.fordham.edu/halsall/basis/peteralex.asp (accessed March 3, 2014). The introductory notes observe that many accounts exist in Coptic, Greek, and Latin, and that these vary in details.

[7] *Catholic Encyclopedia,* s.v. "St. Peter of Alexandria."

[8] William J. Walsh, *The Apparitions and Shrines of Heaven's Bright Queen* (New York: Cary-Stafford, 1906), 1:141.

[9] *Catholic Encyclopedia,* s.v. "St. Catherine of Alexandria."

[10] *Catholic Encyclopedia,* s.v. "St. Jerome." Various sources offer different birth dates, from 340 to 347.

[11] "Letter XXII: To Eustochium," in *Nicene and Post-Nicene Fathers of the Christian Church, Second Series,* ed. Philip Schaff (Edinburgh: T & T Clark: 1886–1900), para. 30, also published at http://www.newadvent.org/fathers/3001022.htm (accessed March 3, 2014).

[12] Ibid., para. 30.

[13] Walsh, *Apparitions and Shrines,* 1:126.

[14] Ibid., 139.

[15] Ibid., 149.

[16] *Catholic Encyclopedia,* s.v. "St. Barbara."

[17] Brewer, *Dictionary,* 416.

[18] *Catholic Encyclopedia,* s.v. "St. Porphory."

[19] Brewer, *Dictionary,* 325.

[20] Marcus Deaconus, *The Life of Saint Porphyry: Bishop of Gaza,* trans. G. F. Hill (Oxford: Clarendon Press, 1913), chap. 7.

[21] Ted Harrison, *Stigmata: A Medieval Mystery in a Modern Age* (New York: St. Martin's Press, 1994), 109.

[22] Karen M. Feaver, "What Chinese Christians taught a U.S. congressional delegation," *Christianity Today,* 38.6 (May 16, 1994), 34. Feaver was part of this delegation that visited China in January 1994, according to the article. She did not report where and when the reported incident occurred.

[23] Walsh, *Apparitions and Shrines*, 2:285.

[24] H. A. Baker, *Visions Beyond the Veil* (Monroeville, Penn.: Whitaker, 1973).

[25] Brewer, *Dictionary*, 19.

[26] *Catholic Encyclopedia*, s.v. "St. Honore."

[27] Brewer, *Dictionary*, 20.

[28] Walsh, *Apparitions and Shrines*, 1:249.

[29] Brewer, *Dictionary*, 62.

[30] *Dialogues*, trans. O.J. Zimmerman (New York: Fathers of the Church, 1959), 2:1.

[31] Brewer, *Dictionary*, 63.

[32] Brewer, *Dictionary*, 297.

[33] Walsh, *Apparitions and Shrines*, 2:53f. The name "Nonnatus," which means "no birth," was acquired because he was delivered by caesarian section.

[34] Walsh, *Apparitions and Shrines*, 1:226–27. *The Catholic Encyclopedia*, in its article on Constance, reports that he was bishop from 934 to 975 and was known as a friend of the poor. He was canonized in 1123.

[35] No entry on this Robert of Lyons is included in *The Catholic Encyclopedia*.

[36] Brewer, *Dictionary*, 325.

[37] *Catholic Encyclopedia*, s.v. "William of Vercelli."

[38] Walsh, *Apparitions and Shrines*, 1:264.

[39] This church, also known as "St. Mary's in the Capitol," is an eleventh-century church in the old town of Cologne, Germany.

[40] This description is from *The Catholic Encyclopedia*, s.v. "Hermann Joseph."

[41] Walsh, *Apparitions and Shrines*, 1:314f.

[42] Ibid., 2:34.

[43] Ibid., 2:11.

[44] *Catholic Encyclopedia*, s.v. "St. Rose of Viterbo."

[45] Brewer, *Dictionary*, 20.

[46] Walsh, *Apparitions and Shrines*, 2:109f.

[47] Ibid., 2:110.

[48] Ibid., 2:127ff.

[49] Ibid., 2:133.

[50] Ibid., 2:134.

[51] Ibid., 2:147f.

[52] Ibid., 1:206.

[53] *Catholic Encyclopedia*, s.v. "Blessed Angela."

[54] *Catholic Encyclopedia*, s.v. "St. Alexis Falconieri."

[55] Walsh, *Apparitions and Shrines,* 2:69.

[56] *Catholic Encyclopedia,* s.v. "St. Bridget of Sweden."

[57] Walsh, *Apparitions and Shrines,* 2:181ff.

[58] Ibid., 2:186.

[59] *Catholic Encyclopedia,* s.v. "St. Catherine of Siena."

[60] Walsh, *Apparitions and Shrines,* 2:189f.

[61] Brewer, *Dictionary,* 20–21.

[62] *Catholic Encyclopedia,* s.v. "St. Vincent Ferrier."

[63] Walsh, *Apparitions and Shrines,* 2:211f.

CHAPTER 3

VISIONS FROM LATE MEDIEVAL TIMES

The question of whether visions or appearances are anything more than hallucinations has been a matter of dispute for some centuries. In a journal entry on May 25, 1768, the famous English preacher John Wesley expressed regret because the English in general and most educated Europeans, including many who believed the Bible, had "given up all accounts of . . . apparitions, as mere old wives' fables." Wesley observed that "if but one account of the intercourse of men with separate spirits be admitted, their whole castle in the air—deism, atheism, materialism—falls to the ground."[1]

Janice Connell describes the significance of recent reports of appearances by the Virgin Mary at Medjugorje in Eastern Europe in similar terms: "The great illusion that the world of the senses is the only reality is gradually being eroded by the shared testimonies . . . of spiritual realities so powerful that people are willing to give their reputations, their fortunes, even their lives, in defense of a transcendent reality they claim they have experienced."[2] The last six centuries have seen a sizable number of reports of visions and appearances of Jesus, and so the modern period continues what had been a feature of the experience of the Church since its earliest days.

Julian of Norwich (Fifteenth Century)

The account that Julian of Norwich has given of her visionary experience that occurred in about 1450 consists of sixteen "shewings" or revelations that took place over several days, as Julian was overcome with an illness that almost took her life. A priest was summoned to administer the last rites of the church, because her death was thought to be imminent. He came with a crucifix, and as she fixed her eyes on it, her "shewings" began. Julian describes the onset of the visions as follows: "Suddenly I saw the red blood running down from under the garland, hot and fresh, plenteous and life-like, just as it was in the time that the garland of thorns was pressed down on his blessed head."[3]

Julian's account has become a classic in visionary literature because of its detailed description of the sufferings of Jesus and her reflections on her experience. Critics are at odds about whether these were only vividly imagined pictures or whether she saw something with her own eyes, and questions have also been raised about Julian's own understanding of them.

Julian says this revelation was shown in three parts: "by bodily sight, by words formed in my understanding, and by ghostly sight. But the ghostly sight I cannot or may not shew it as clearly and as fully as I would."[4] In her account, Julian says that as she looked at the crucifix her sight began to fail, the room around her grew dark as night except for a mysterious light that remained around the crucifix, and the pain left her body. As she continued to look at the crucifix, she saw red blood trickling down from under the crown of thorns on the head of Jesus. When the blood reached his brows, it vanished. This vision of flowing blood continued for a while, during which time she received insights into the significance of the suffering of Jesus. She says enough blood was running from the thorns on his head to make her whole bed red, but this did not occur because the blood continued to vanish. This detail helps us understand a little more about the nature of her experience and explains why some critics have believed her experience was an imaginative vision.

Julian offers some insight into her understanding of what she calls "ghostly sight," describing Jesus as showing her a ghostly sight of his loving character[5] and being given a ghostly sight of Mary as high, noble, and glorious.[6] She points out that she wished to see Mary in bodily presence but did not. On another occasion, she reports having had her "ghostly eye" opened so that she might see her own soul in the midst of her heart as an endless world and a blissful kingdom.[7]

The extraordinary character of visions evidently presents challenges for those who experience them to describe them adequately, and ordinary language often becomes strained in those descriptions. We still speak figuratively about "seeing with the eyes of the soul," and Julian seems to be using that kind of idiom in her account.

Julian also describes another kind of visionary experience seemingly between the bodily and ghostly sights, describing a "shewing" that was "full mistily . . . of a Lord that hath a servant;" at the same time her understanding was illumined.[8] She says that one part was "shewed ghostly in bodily likeness, and the other part was shewed more ghostly, without bodily likeness."[9] I do not have a clear understanding of what difference she saw between the two kinds of experience described earlier but will comment more in later chapters on the strange perceptions visionaries sometimes report. One of the important questions related to visionary experiences is if any of them allow us to draw conclusions about whether forms of reality exist beyond the ones we encounter in everyday sense experience.

Blessed Osanna of Mantua, Italy (Fifteenth Century)

Osanna was born in Mantua to wealthy parents; when she was six, her family spent the summer in the country.[10] As Osanna wandered alone on the meadow one day, an angel appeared to her and told her about the love of God. Soon afterward, Jesus met her in the same spot in the form of a lovely child, bearing a heavy cross and wearing a crown of thorns. He told her he was the son of the Virgin Mary and the Creator, and that he loved all children. Osanna responded by consecrating herself to him.

Although many visionaries have reported seeing Jesus as a child, seldom does he seem to have appeared as child undergoing suffering. Among the experiences that marked Osanna's religious life were stigmata that appeared on her body, and she was known during her life for prayer, works of charity, and spiritual experiences in which she entered into the sufferings of Jesus Christ.

The source for Osanna's reported experience at six years of age, given that she was alone when it happened, must have been Osanna herself. We might wonder about the ability of a six-year-old child to differentiate between an actual encounter and a reverie that is taken for reality in the remembering and the retelling. The challenge in approaching this and other similar accounts, in my opinion, is being neither too gullible nor too critical. We will never know the extent of human experience in all its variety unless we patiently listen. However, not everyone describes events close to the way they transpired. Beliefs, expectations, and previous experiences all influence what we notice and what we report. Besides this, of course, some people are dishonest, and others are too confused or deluded to give reliable reports. But the fact that someone's account *might* be flawed does not establish that it *is* flawed. Skepticism needs to be kept in check, although it should have some place in evaluating reports. I consider some six-year-old children as having the capacity to supply authoritative reports.

Brother Ernest of Clifton, England (Fifteenth Century)

Ernest of Clifton, England, gave away his inheritance to the poor in 1430 in order to become a monk. His devotion so impressed his abbot that when their city was attacked by the plague, the abbot commanded Ernest to pray before the altar of Mary until he received an answer. She answered, directing Ernest to say certain prayers, and the plague ceased. After this, Ernest was assailed by temptation and eventually left the monastic life to satisfy his immoral desires. One form of depravity led to another, and he finally settled on operating an inn, stealing from and murdering travelers who lodged with him. One night he entered a room to murder its occupant, but found himself looking at Jesus, full of the wounds of crucifixion. Jesus looked at him in pity and asked, "Do you wish to kill me again? Stretch forth your hand and murder me again." Ernest was so moved by this experience that he confessed all his doings to the authorities, who sentenced him to hang without even giving him time to make confession to a priest. He is said to have been rescued from execution by Mary herself, and upon being freed, returned to monastic life.[11]

Blessed Lucy (Fifteenth Century)

Lucy of Narni, Italy, was born to a noble family; from earliest childhood she played with pious objects, including a statue of the infant Jesus. When she was seven, Lucy went to visit the home of her uncle, which included a room with angels painted on the ceiling. She wanted to be alone in that room but found the staircase was too steep to climb. She is said to have appealed to Jesus for help and miraculously found herself in the room. While she prayed there, she was given a vision of Jesus, accompanied by his Mother, Saints Dominic, Catherine of Siena, and other saints and angels. Jesus then espoused her to himself, placing a precious ring on her finger. Saint Dominic then gave her the scapular of his order, which she wore under her clothes until she was able to wear it in public. Lucy, who was marked later in life with the stigmata, died in 1544.[12]

Catherine of Bologna (Fifteenth Century)

Catherine was born into a noble Italian family in 1413 and placed in the court of Princess Elizabeth at Ferrara at the age of eleven. She chose to enter the convent of Saint Clare, however, and later founded one in Bologna. Catherine was chosen abbess of the community in her native town, an office that she held until her death in 1463.[13] She was beset by persistent temptations in the early days of her religious life but in later years enjoyed the heights of contemplation. Her instructions on the spiritual life are to be found in her "Treatise on the Seven Spiritual Weapons," which also contains an account of her own struggles.

Catherine was tested by false apparitions and terrible temptations, but after overcoming them went on to serve her sisters.[14] Several saints appeared to her, including Saint Thomas of Canterbury. Jesus appeared to her as well, once to take note of the hymn she was singing, and another time in the form of a child. She died in 1463, and her body is said not to have undergone decay.

Stephana Quinzani (Fifteenth Century)

Stephana was born in 1457 near Brescia in Italy; her family was devout, and Stephana herself took vows of poverty and chastity at the age of seven.[15] Christ is said to have then appeared to her, accompanied by the Virgin Mary, Saints Dominic, Thomas Aquinas, and Catherine of Siena, and then espoused himself to her, giving her a ring that was seen by many people. She experienced another encounter some time later, after entirely renouncing her own will to do the will of God. Jesus appeared to her and said, "My daughter, since of the love of Me you have generously stripped yourself of your own will, ask what you will and I will grant it to you." Her reply was, "I desire nothing but yourself, O Lord."[16]

Blessed Magdalen Pannatieri (Fifteenth Century)

Magdalen was born in Trino, in northern Italy, in 1443. After receiving a good education, she entered religious life, taking Saints Dominic and Catharine of Siena as her models of holiness. She fasted, practiced flagellation, and spent long periods in fervent prayer. She was honored with frequent appearances, and her face is said to have shone with celestial light during one Easter week. The Virgin Mary often appeared to her, placing the child Jesus in her arms.

Walsh reports that she was frequently visited by Saints Peter and Paul, and that she was also "taken in spirit" many times to Israel and could make minute and accurate descriptions of the places she saw.[17] Prophecies and miracles are also attributed to her. Just before her death in 1503, she reported to friends that Jesus and his Mother, accompanied by several saints, had come to visit her. She knew this to be a signal that her time to die had come. Wonderful fragrances are said to have perfumed the air as this happy event transpired.

This account is interesting for the many marvelous phenomena associated with the life of Magdalen. Prophecy, strange fragrances, teleportation, and other things have often been reported along with visual encounters with Jesus. They suggest that "another world" exists, of which humans are often only dimly aware, if at all. Encounters with Jesus in the twentieth century have also been reported as occurring in the context of other marvels.

Saint Ignatius de Loyola (Sixteenth Century)

Ignatius is best-known for having established the Jesuit Order.[18] He was born in 1491 at the castle of Loyola in Spain and later took the name Ignatius when he was living in Rome. He admits living a dissolute life as a young man, until an experience in 1521 that happened while he was recovering from a wound in his leg made by a cannon ball. He began to ponder living in service to God, when he saw

> the image of Our Lady with the Holy Child Jesus, at whose sight for a notable time he felt a reassuring sweetness, which eventually left him with such a loathing of his past sins, and especially for those of the flesh, that every unclean imagination seemed blotted out from his soul, and never again was there the least consent to any carnal thought.[19]

A period of penance followed, including a time when he considered suicide, which led him to resolve to neither eat nor drink until God gave him peace, which finally came. His notes on his experiences at this time eventually became the basis for the Ignatian spiritual exercises.

Ignatius drew a band of followers around him, who vowed in 1534 to be poor, chaste, and as much like Jesus as possible. In 1541, at the time that the small group of priests who joined him in his efforts to develop a religious order had voted him the superior, Jesus appeared to him again. After Ignatius had said Mass at Saint Paul's Basilica in Rome and vowed to lead the new order, he entered a chapel to pray, and Jesus appeared to him bearing his cross. Then God the Father commended Ignatius to the care of his Son with the words,

"Receive this man as Thy servant." Jesus then turned to Ignatius and said, "I will be favourable to you in Rome."[20]

Ignatius died of Roman fever in 1556; by that time, the company he formed already had 1,000 members.

Blessed Dominica (Sixteenth Century)

In 1525, when Dominica of Florence, Italy, was only ten years old, she saw a beautiful woman holding by the hand a child whose feet and breast were wounded. Dominica asked who had wounded the child, and its mother replied, "Love." Dominica had earlier placed flowers from her garden before an image of Mary, and the Child took those flowers and laid them on the head of Dominica. She then recognized Mary and the Child and prostrated herself before them.[21]

Teresa of Avila (Sixteenth Century)

Teresa of Avila was a nun of the Carmelite order and prioress of the Discalced (or shoeless) Carmelites. The experiences in which Jesus appeared took place over a number of years, according to her account in *The Life of the Holy Mother Teresa of Jesus*. She also reports experiences in which diabolical agencies sought her destruction and some appearances from heavenly visitors.

Teresa's experiences have been widely examined by scholars in recent years, and many have concluded that experiences such as these point to mental disorders of one kind or another. Hysteria has often been suggested; more recently, it has been theorized that she suffered from a disorder in which important memories and conflicts stemming from very early childhood, and even birth, are relived, often with much pain and physical contortions. However, a Canadian scholar has recently defended an interpretation of Teresa's experiences that does not attribute any mental illness to her at all.[22] People reporting visions and apparitions are often said to be mentally ill, but such diagnoses can perhaps be questioned when people interact well with others, hold down jobs, and in other ways are normal.

Teresa often provides us with detailed accounts of what she saw in her encounters. One of these she describes this way:

> I saw Christ at my side—or, to put it better, I was conscious of Him, for I saw nothing with the eyes of the body or the eyes of the soul. He seemed quite close to me, and I saw that it was He. . . . Being completely ignorant that such visions were possible, I was very much afraid at first. . . . All the time Jesus Christ seemed to be by my side, but as this was not an imaginary vision I could not see in what form. But I most clearly felt that He was all the time on my right, and was a witness of everything that I was doing.[23]

The detail that Teresa offers, oddly enough, has contributed to the debate over the nature of her experiences. In one place, for instance, she writes about seeing the hands of Jesus:

> By the mere beauty and whiteness of a single one of the hands which we are shown the imagination is completely transcended. In any case, there is no other way in which it would be possible for us to see in a moment things of which we have no recollection, when we have never thought of, and which, even in a long period of time, we could not invent with our imagination, because, as I have already said, they far transcend what we can comprehend on earth.[24]

Teresa indicates her eagerness to show that her experiences were genuine, not just the work of her imagination. Visionaries frequently confront the accusation that they do not really see anything but have overactive imaginations. Teresa also was accused of having experiences whose origins were diabolical, and this accusation is also made today.

Scholars still debate whether she saw Jesus with "the eyes of the body," or with "the eyes of the soul." Teresa writes at one point:

> At times it certainly seemed to me as if I were looking at a painting, but on many other occasions it appeared to be no painting but Christ Himself, such was the clarity with which He was pleased to appear to me. Yet there were times when the vision was so indistinct that I did think it was a painting, although it bore no resemblance even to the most perfect of earthly pictures.[25]

In another place, she describes how, in a time of greater spiritual distress, she saw Christ above her in the air: "I raised my eyes to the sky and saw Christ—not in Heaven, but far above me in the air—holding out His hand towards me."[26] Again, this description leaves the strong impression that she did not consider this experience imaginary.

Teresa's visions culminate in an experience in which an angel took a golden spear with a fiery iron tip and pierced her heart so deeply that it penetrated her entrails. The description of her visions as only intellectual ones, which I mentioned in the previous chapter as being the view of the author of the article in *The Catholic Encyclopedia*, is too simplistic.

Saint Alphonsus Rodriguez (Sixteenth Century)

Alphonsus (or Alonso) was born in Segovia, Spain in 1532, the son of a wool merchant who had been reduced to poverty.[27] After the death of his wife and three children, he determined to enter the Jesuit order, and was admitted as a lay-brother because he lacked the education to be a Jesuit.

His mother taught him the life of devotion, and even from an early age he exhibited intense love for Mary.[28] Upon giving himself to a life of devotion to God, he was in constant sorrow over his sins. One night the Lord appeared to him with a number of saints, all surrounded by glory. Among these saints was Saint Francis, who approached Alphonsus and asked him why he wept so much. He replied that he found even a single sin to require repentance with weeping. This reply is said to have pleased the Lord, who looked at him in love and then disappeared.

Alphonsus, who died in 1617, is known for his life of contemplation on the passion of Christ.

Catharine of Raconigi, Italy (Sixteenth Century)

Catharine was born to very poor parents, but experienced divine favor from a very early age. When she was five, she broke a cup that her mother greatly valued. As she wept in fear of being punished, a beautiful child is said to have suddenly appeared in the room; he picked up the broken pieces, restored the cup to her whole, then vanished.[29] Also at this age, Catharine was espoused by the Virgin Mary to the Infant Jesus, in the presence of many angels and saints. These espousals were renewed on two subsequent occasions.

Catharine lived as a poor peasant woman, working hard for herself and her family. On one occasion, as she tearfully prayed to God to help her family in their poverty and misery, a child as destitute as she appeared, begging for alms. She said she had nothing to give him. The child then made himself known to her as Jesus. He gave her some money for food and encouraged her to bear her poverty cheerfully, just as he had done. After a life of self-renunciation, she died at the age of sixty-two.

Saint Cajetan of Lombardy (Sixteenth Century)

Cajetan (or Gaetano) was born in 1480 near Venice and studied law at the famous University of Padua as a young man. He was appointed to serve the Roman Curia and spent his personal fortune to build hospitals and relieve those who suffered. He finally entered the priesthood and developed the order of Theatins, which vowed to own no property and to avoid asking alms, believing that the providence of God would supply their wants.

Cajetan, who was dedicated from his infancy to Mary, was fascinated by the mystery of the Incarnation and contemplated it often.[30] At Christmas, in 1517, he was again moved by the birth of Jesus as he worshipped before the altar of the crib. He wanted to ask Mary to lay the baby in his arms but felt unworthy of such an honor. As he contemplated this desire, Saints Jerome and Joseph appeared to him, urging him to hold out his arms. As he did so, Mary appeared, and laid the Child Jesus in his arms.

He passed the last four years of his life in Naples where he died in 1547, suffering in his last moments a kind of mystical crucifixion.[31]

Saint Stanislaus Kostka (Sixteenth Century)

Stanislaus was born into one of the leading families of Poland in 1550 and brought up in a strict home.[32] He was sent, along with his brother and a tutor, to a Jesuit college in Vienna in 1564, where he exhibited an unconscious reverence that fascinated all the young men in the college. He is said to have been often raised from the ground in ecstasy, and to have tried to conceal his fervor from his companions. The Jesuit college was disbanded soon after Stanislaus arrived in Vienna, and the brothers and several other students went to live with a Lutheran gentleman in the fashionable quarter of the city. Stanislaus was the only one with religious devotion, however, and was the object of ridicule for it. His brother would often beat him, and reproach him for "living the life of a country clown instead of that of a gentleman."[33]

In 1566 Stanislaus became ill, and in a delirium saw a vision of a large black dog that leaped on his bed to attack him. Three times he drove it away by the sign of the cross. Because he thought death was imminent, he asked for the last rites, but no Catholic priest was allowed to cross the threshold of a Protestant landlord. However, Stanislaus knew that the power to obtain the last sacrament for the dying was attributed to Saint Barbara, and on one occasion reported to his tutor that she was in the room with two angels, bringing him Holy Communion. That night, he later reported, the Virgin had appeared with the Divine Child. She placed the Child on his bed, and they caressed and embraced each other. Mary then instructed him to enter the Jesuit order.

As he neared his death from a fever in 1568, he wrote a letter to the Virgin Mary, begging her to call him to the skies to celebrate with her the glorious anniversary of her Assumption.[34] His confidence is considered to have been rewarded, for when he died, his face shone with the most serene light. The entire city of Rome proclaimed him a saint and people hastened from all parts to venerate his remains and to obtain, if possible, some relics.

Thomas Michaelek (Sixteenth Century)

Thomas was born in Lezajsk, Poland, and was known as a simple but pious man.[35] He was gathering wood for his fire one day, at a place where he often prayed, when he saw Jesus with his mother and father. Mary spoke to him, saying, "Thomas, I have chosen this place; on it my Son will be honored, and everyone who shall invoke me here shall experience my intercession. Go to the rulers of the city and tell them that it is my will and command, and also that of my Son, that they build here a church dedicated to me."

Thomas was too humble to consider himself a recipient of a heavenly vision, so he kept the revelation secret, fearing that he might have experienced a diabolical deception. Twice he was reminded by Mary about the request, and he finally asked the city rulers if he might set up a cross where the vision had taken place. Soon people from his community began to gather at the spot to pray, and their prayers were answered. Sometime later, another inhabitant, Sebastian Talarczyk, saw Mary dressed in white and surrounded by light at the spot where Thomas had put up the cross. He went to the city rulers and reported what he had seen, and they authorized the building of a church on that site.

Peter de Basto (Seventeenth Century)

Peter de Basto was born to the illustrious family of Machado in Portugal,[36] with prospects of a brilliant career. But this was not his destiny. Like many people who are favored with divine visitations, his experiences began in childhood. While praying in church one day, he saw "with the eyes of the body," in the words of Walsh, many angels near the altar. This experience caused Peter to become interested in spiritual matters. In his late teens he joined the military and left for the West Indies. But his ship was wrecked on the way, and for five days he was tossed about in the sea. During this time, Mary and Jesus appeared to him, and he consequently devoted himself to religious service for the rest of his life and joined the Jesuits as a lay brother.

Peter was once sent on a pilgrimage with two young companions and was instructed to beg from village to village, rather than accept hospitality from members of the Order. One day they met a family consisting of an old man, a woman, and a little child, who received him very kindly and insisted that they eat a frugal meal together. When the family indicated their desire to depart, Peter pressed them for their names. The mother replied that they were the three founders of the Society of Jesus, "and all three disappeared at the same instant."[37] This experience resembles the accounts of the gospels in which Jesus disappeared, but it includes his mother and earthly father, which is not found in any Gospel accounts.

Before his death in 1645, Peter asked God for the gift of patience in suffering. In response, Peter was allowed to see Jesus covered with wounds, a purple mantle around his shoulders, a rope around his neck, a reed in his hand, and a crown of thorns upon his head. He told Peter that it was in this way that "the true Son of God has suffered to teach men how to suffer."

Saint Margaret Mary Alacoque (Seventeenth Century)

Margaret was born at Lautecourt, France, in 1647 into a noble family, and at the age of four began to be instructed in Christian faith by her godmother.[38] At an early age, she was aware of the presence of Christ in the Holy Sacrament, and soon after became aware of his presence "that was palpable to her senses and not only to her soul."[39] He would often present himself as crucified or as carrying the cross, which increased a desire in her to participate in his sufferings. She describes these manifestations of himself as ones in which he did not appear in person, which she found difficult to describe: "I see him," she writes, "I feel him near me, and I hear him much better than I could with my bodily senses."[40]

When Margaret was seventeen, her mother encouraged her to establish herself in the world.[41] She thought the childhood vows of devotion Margaret had made were not binding and believed she could serve God at home by penance and charity to the poor. So Margaret began to take part in the pleasures of the world. One night upon her return from a ball, she had a vision of Christ as he was being scourged. He reproached her for infidelity after having given her so many proofs of his love. During her entire life, Margaret mourned over two faults committed at this time—wearing of some superfluous ornaments and a mask at the carnival to please her brothers.

At twenty-six, Margaret entered the convent of Paray, and vowed to stay in the life of devotion, including suffering, that was her destiny. In 1673 she had a revelation of the love of Christ that has been passed to many. She says that he appeared to her and said,

> My Divine Heart is so passionately in love with men that it can no longer contain within itself the flames of its ardent charity. It must pour them out by means of thee, and manifest itself to them to enrich them with its precious treasures, which contain all the graces of which they have need to be saved from perdition. I have chosen thee as an abyss of unworthiness and ignorance to accomplish so great a design, so that all may be done by Me.[42]

He then asked Margaret for her heart, and she gave it to him. He then put it into his own heart, which felt to her as though it had been placed into a fiery furnace. He then drew it out and gave it back to her, and said:

> Behold, my beloved, a precious proof of my love. I enclose in thy heart a little spark of the most ardent flame of My love to serve thee as a heart, and to consume thee till thy last moment. Until now thou hast taken only the name of my slave; henceforth thou shalt be called the well–beloved disciple of My Sacred Heart.[43]

She reports that he revealed his heart to her in subsequent apparitions as a sun brilliant with sparkling light, the burning rays of which fell directly on her heart and enflamed it. Margaret introduced the devotion to the Sacred Heart of Jesus to Catholic Christians and died in 1690.

Saint Rose of Lima, Peru (Seventeenth Century)

Rose, born in 1586, was named Isabel at her baptism, but a beautiful rose is said to have appeared in the air over her cradle, gently touching her face and then disappearing.[44] Rose, as she was subsequently called, began a life of devotion to God when still a young girl.

Her mother died when Rose was still young, and the woman her father subsequently married and the children born of this second marriage mistreated Rose. Her solace was her faith, and the visitations of the child Jesus, which are said to have occurred daily for some time, and to have been witnessed by others. Walsh reports: "If by midday she had not yet received a visit from her Heavenly Guest, she would implore Him with sighs and tears to come to her, and would send her Guardian Angel to invite him."[45] Like many other saints whose lives have been described for us, Rose experienced the assaults of the devil. On one occasion after being tempted to impurity, she scourged herself with an iron chain and asked the Lord why she had been abandoned. As she asked the question, he appeared to her, looked at her in love and informed her that she had been able to conquer the temptation because he was in her heart. On another occasion he appeared to her in a vision between two arches, one of which was brilliant with color, and the other of which had the blood-stained cross at its center. She was led to understand that the arches signified glory and sufferings, respectively, and that heavenly joys find their source in earthly sorrows. Rose died in 1617 at the age of 31 and was canonized as a saint in 1671 by Pope Clement X.

Benoite Rencurel (Seventeenth Century)

Benoite was born in 1647 in a village of the Laus valley in France. Her family was poor, and after her father died when she was seven, her mother was forced to sell her land to support the family. Benoite became a shepherdess to help earn her living.

Mary first appeared to her when she was only five, and when she was sixteen these visitations began to occur almost daily, and that lasted for fifty-four years. Benoite was instructed to encourage the faithful of the valley to build a sanctuary, and miracles of healing began to occur as soon as it was complete. Benoite was said to be able to discover the hidden sins of people by her sense of smell, and many people were brought back to virtue by her disclosures.

In 1673, while praying before the cross, she was granted a vision of Jesus suffering on the cross. Blood flowed from all his wounds, and he spoke to Benoite, informing her she would suffer the sorrow of his passion. Each week, from Thursday at four until Saturday at nine, Benoite would lie on her bed, her arms extended in the form of a cross, her feet crossed as though nailed to the cross, and her body "as rigid as an iron bar."[46] After some time, the stigmata appeared, and blood flowed from her hands and side. She reported that the pain was excruciating. Jesus often appeared to her to console her during these agonies, which lasted for a period of twenty years. She died peacefully in 1718.

Emanuel Swedenborg (Eighteenth Century)

Swedenborg was an established man of science and letters in Sweden until he was in his fifties, when his life as a visionary began. His experiences span an eighteen- or nineteen-year period (1743–1772) and include several visions of Jesus. On April 6, 1744, he had a dream that he reported in this way: First he heard a roaring noise of many winds; this was followed by a powerful trembling that caused him to shake from head and foot, and then a presence of something indescribably holy which threw him on his face.[47] He exclaimed, "Oh, Almighty Jesus Christ! Thou who of Thy great mercy deignest to come to so great a sinner, make me worthy of this grace!" Upon reflecting on this prayer later, he felt that the words had been put in his mouth. As Swedenborg prayed with his hands folded, a hand came forth and pressed his hands. He found himself "lying in His [Christ's] bosom and beheld Him face to face."

In April 1745, he had a spiritual experience that gave a new direction to his life. Our knowledge of it does not come from Swedenborg's voluminous writings, ironically, but from a verbatim account written down by a friend. As Swedenborg finished his midday meal, he noticed a dimness before his eyes. It grew darker, and then he saw the floor covered with crawling creatures such as snakes and frogs. The narrative in Swedenborg's own words continues:

> The darkness prevailed, and then suddenly it dispersed and I saw a man sitting in a corner of the room ... [who] said, "Eat not so much!" Again all became black before my eyes, but immediately it cleared away and I found myself alone in the room. . . . I went to my room, but that night the same man revealed himself to me again. I was not frightened then. He said that he was the Lord God, the Creator and Redeemer of the world.[48]

Swedenborg reported that he saw the Lord seated near his bed in imperial purple and majestic light, and that the light did not affect his eyes. Swedenborg devoted his labors to spiritual things from that day on.

Swedenborg makes several references in his *Spiritual Diary* to experiences in which he saw Christ. He says that he saw Jesus while asleep "with the face and form in which He had been when He was in the world."[49] Swedenborg goes on to say that when he awakened he still saw Jesus, although obscurely, and was told that such had been his earthly appearance. This event took place on the night of November 18, 1751, and so is distinct from the dream account noted above. Having a vision begin during sleep and continue after a person wakes is certainly a peculiar phenomenon, but some sense of the range of Swedenborg's experiences can be gleaned from reflecting on the four kinds of "sight" or "vision" distinguished by Swedenborg.[50]

The first is sight that takes place during sleep but is as vivid as that which occurs when awake. "The second is vision with closed eyes, which is as vivid as when the eyes are open." He goes on to remark that the second kind of vision could also occur when one's eyes are open. The third kind of vision occurs when the eyes are open, and things in heaven, including spirits, are represented. He describes this kind of vision as rather obscure, and as differing completely from the ordinary experience of imagination. The fourth kind occurs when a person is separated from his or her body, but has the sense of being awake. He says that in this state a person enjoys all senses, including touch, hearing, and sight, and in a way that exceeds sense experience during wakefulness. Swedenborg's classification bears little resemblance to Augustine's classical threefold account of corporeal, imaginative, and intellectual visions.

Perhaps only a person who has had extensive visionary experience could appreciate the distinctions Swedenborg draws between different kinds of visions. In my research on visions, I have met people whose dreams of divine encounters were interpreted as having as much reality as a perceptual experience that might occur during waking life. I also met a person whose experience began during a dream and continued after awaking, another for whom having eyes open or closed made no difference concerning what he saw, and yet another whose experience began while she was awake and then continued in what resembled an out-of-the-body experience.

Evidence from first-hand accounts suggests that no simple classification of vision or apparition experiences is plausible. Augustine's three-fold classification stems from a time in which theological views—such as that which construes a human to consist of a tripartite division of body, soul, and spirit—were allowed to override observation. However, exact studies in the last few centuries, including that which is undertaken by various sciences, have honed skills of observation so that more attention is given to empirical detail. Consequently, the world is a complex place, and and the language used to explain and describe the human experience has become more complex.

Blessed Anne Catherine Emmerich
(Eighteenth Century)

Catherine was born in 1774 in Flamske, near Munster, Germany, to a poor country family, and from childhood she was known for her pious conduct.[51] Jesus as a child is said to have played with her, and the Virgin Mary also appeared often to her. When she herded sheep, she would frequently be visited by the Good Shepherd, in the form of a young shepherd.[52] While still a young woman, she sought to enter a convent but could not do so, apparently because of her poor estate.

When Catherine was twenty-four, Jesus appeared to her as she knelt in prayer before a crucifix in the Jesuit church at Koesfeld.[53] He appeared as a heavenly young bridegroom and walked toward her. In his right hand he held a crown of flowers, and in his left a crown of thorns, and he offered these to Catherine that she might make her choice. She seized the crown of thorns that had been on his head, and with both hands pressed it upon her own head. The vision came to an end, but the pains that ensued never left her. During the next

Passion week, the crown of thorns became visible, and blood flowed through her head-dress.

The Augustinian convent at Dulmen allowed her to enter in 1802, but she found the devotion practiced there to be inconsistent with the rigors she personally undertook. Consequently, she was misunderstood and accused of vanity and hypocrisy but bore her opposition in silence. In 1812 she received the stigmata as she contemplated the sufferings of Christ and asked to share in them. As she prayed, she saw a light descending from above, and in the middle of it was the living crucified Lord, who approached with his wounds shining like five bright rays of light. These rays of light then pierced her hands, feet, and side, as though they were arrows proceeding from him. After that she wanted nothing but the Blessed Sacrament, until she passed away on February 9, 1824. Among the marvels attributed to her was foreseeing the downfall of Napoleon twelve years in advance.[54]

Apparitions at Castelpetroso, Italy (Nineteenth Century)

The apparitions at Castelpetroso primarily involve the Virgin Mary, but the dead body of Jesus is also said to have been seen there, and so I include it. Two women in their thirties, who were herding sheep, reported in 1888 that they had seen a light coming from some fissures in rocks. Upon approaching the spot, they saw a young, pale, disheveled, but beautiful lady, "bleeding from the wounds received from seven swords."[55] No one paid attention to these reports at first, but various other people, including a heretic, reported that they saw the Mother of Dolors, as this appearance of Mary is called, bearing her dead Son in her arms. Pilgrimages to the site began, so that within a few days 4,000 people had visited the spot. Many reported seeing Mary, although the appearances of her varied. She was generally seen alone, but on some occasions was seen with Saint Michael or troops of angels, or with one of the saints, including Saints Anthony and Sebastian. One of the priests, who initially did not believe in the apparitions but went to see for himself, reported as follows:

> I had many times derided those who visited the mountain on which these wondrous Apparitions took place. On May 16, 1888, however, more to pass the time than for anything else, I felt a desire to visit the place. When I arrived I began to look into one of the fissures, and I saw with great clearness Our Lady, like a statuette, with a little Child in her arms. After a short interval I looked again at the same spot; and, in place of the Most Holy Virgin I saw, quite clearly, the dead Saviour bearing the cross of thorns and all covered with blood.[56]

Various other marvelous events have been reported from this site, including healing cures.

General Booth (Nineteenth Century)

General Booth is best known for establishing the Salvation Army mission to the poor more than a century ago. He is reported to have had a vision in which he saw a myriad of angelic beings as well as patriarchs, apostles, and Christian martyrs. Then he saw Jesus, who rebuked him for his "nominal, useless, lazy, professing Christian life."[57] This experience led to the establishment of the well-known mission.

Sadhu Sundar Singh (Twentieth Century)

Sundar Singh of India had a vision experience in 1903, when he was fourteen, after an encounter with Christians who gave him a New Testament to read.[58] As an expression of contempt for what they believed, he burned the book in public. Three days later, he had the vision that changed his life's direction. A bright cloud filled his room, and out of the cloud came the face and figure of Jesus, who spoke to him.[59] As a consequence, Singh converted to Christianity, but he donned the robe and lived the life common to the sadhus of India. His extraordinary approach to Christian faith attracted a large following in the early part of the twentieth century, including the people of Europe to whom he spoke.

Dangers of Apparitions

Walsh includes some interesting commentary from Fr. R. F. Clarke, about the dangers of apparitions. Clarke warns his readers about the possibility that such apparitions might have their source in the demonic world and observes that "the one great ambition of the devil is to secure for himself the worship that is due to God alone."[60] Clarke instructs his readers to avoid hasty judgment about the source of visions, and offers guidance for evaluating such experiences. He notes that events brought about by God have lasting good effects, and observes that the apparitions of Mary at Lourdes satisfy this requirement. He hesitates to endorse the apparitions of Mary at Tilley, for the visions there have sometimes been followed by faintness, loss of consciousness, and a morbid physical condition. By contrast, he says, divine visitations bring joy, peace of mind, and health of both body and soul. He also expresses concerns over the varying, shifting nature of the vision at Tilley, for Mary is sometimes seen alone, and at other times is seen carrying Jesus in her arms; sometimes her whole figure is seen, and at other times only her head and shoulders are seen; and sometimes a luminous cloud has gradually developed into human form. Clarke notes, however, that these facts should not be considered proof against the reality of the visions. Clarke's guidelines are no doubt useful, although they are probably difficult to apply, as the following account suggests.

In 1996 I made a presentation on my research into visions of Jesus at a conference held at Harvard Divinity School, and after my talk a professor of religious studies at an eastern American university came up to me to discuss my research. He said he had been converted through such a vision while in Ireland. He reported that he sat for an hour or so in a grotto at one of the holy wells in Ireland, and various persons appeared to him as apparitions, including Padre Pia, the Virgin Mary, and Jesus. His wife was also in the grotto, but she was not sitting with him. When they left the grotto together, he told her what he had just seen, and the exact order in which they appeared (not necessarily what I have just listed). She told him she had seen the same apparitions and in the same order. He told me this experience resulted in his conversion to Christianity from being "just a pagan." He also reported that his wife became depressed after this incident, and for a long time wished to go to Medjugore, the site of a spate of Marian apparitions, in order to be healed of her depression. He was initially reluctant to go but eventually gave in to her request, and said his wife was healed at Medjugore.

If we apply Clarke's rule concerning the effects of apparitions to the lives of the professor and his wife, we would probably have to say that the experience in Ireland was positive for him but not for her. This would have a curious consequence, for it would suggest that the apparitions were simultaneously authentic and inauthentic! While I do not discount the value of these guidelines for evaluating the experiences of others, or perhaps even one's own, I suggest that they cannot be applied in a simplistic way.

This completes the representative accounts I will mention of visions of Jesus through the last two millennia. Some accounts from the twentieth century can be found in the book authored by Chester and Lucille Huyssen mentioned above, and Scott Sparrow has reported on visions of Jesus from his psychotherapeutic practice in *I am With You Always: True Stories of Encounters with Jesus.*[61] I will present the results of my own research in the next four chapters and will focus on some of the perceptual details that are seldom provided in the accounts that have been mentioned to this point. I consider these details to be particularly important in trying to assess the significance of these visions, apparitions, appearances, encounters, or whatever they should be called.[62]

I continue to be interested in this remarkable phenomenon, so I invite my readers to supply me with further accounts, and, where possible, references to their sources.

Notes

[1] *The Works of John Wesley, Volume 22: Journal and Diaries V (1765–75)*, eds. W. Reginald Ward and Richard P. Heitzenrater (Nashville, TN: Abingdon Press, 1993), 135.

[2] Janice Connell, *The Visions of the Children: The Apparitions of the Blessed Mother at Medjugorje* (New York: St. Martin's, 1992), xii.

[3] Julian of Norwich, *The Revelations of Divine Love*, trans. J. Walsh (London: Burns & Oates, 1961), chap. 4.

[4] Ibid., chap. 9.

[5] Ibid., chap. 5.

[6] Ibid., chap. 25.

[7] Ibid., chap. 67.

[8] Ibid., chap. 51.

[9] Ibid., chap. 4.

[10] Walsh, *Apparitions and Shrines*, 2:321f.

[11] Ibid., 2:281f.

[12] Walsh, *Apparitions and Shrines*, 2:305f.

[13] *Catholic Encyclopedia*, s.v. "St. Catherine of Bologna."

[14] Walsh, *Apparitions and Shrines*, 2:289.

[15] Ibid., 2:291f.

[16] Ibid., 2:293. I have modified the quote somewhat, as Walsh reported it in Elizabethan English.

[17] Ibid., 2:317f.

[18] *Catholic Encyclopedia*, s.v. "St. Ignatius Loyola."

[19] *Catholic Encyclopedia*, s.v. "St Ignatius Loyola." The account is drawn from his autobiography.

[20] Walsh, *Apparitions and Shrines*, 2:362.

[21] Ibid., 2:373.

[22] Laurence Nixon, "Maladjustment and self-actualization in the life of Teresa of Avila," *Studies in Religion/ Sciences Religieuses* 18 (1989), 283–95.

[23] Saint Teresa of Avila, *The Life of the Holy Mother Teresa of Jesus*, trans. E. Allison Peers (London: Sheed & Ward, 1946), chap. 27.

[24] Ibid., chap. 28

[25] Ibid., chap. 28.

[26] Ibid., chap. 39.

[27] *Catholic Encyclopedia*, s.v. "St. Alphonsus Rodriguez."

[28] Walsh, *Apparitions and Shrines*, 3:59f.

[29] Ibid., 2:313. Walsh expresses no misgivings about this story, even though the source for it must have been the five-year-old child.

[30] Ibid., 2:335f.

[31] *Catholic Encylopedia*, s.v. "St. Cajetan."

[32] Walsh, *Apparitions and Shrines*, 3:41ff.

[33] Ibid., 3:44.

[34] *Catholic Encyclopedia*, s.v. "St. Stanislaus Kostka."

[35] Walsh, *Apparitions and Shrines*, 3:101f.

[36] F. X. Schouppe, *Purgatory: Illustrated in the Lives and Legends of the Saints* (London: Burns, Oates and Washbourne, 1920), chap. 7, para. 141. ("Purgatory, the Mystery of Mercy.")

[37] Walsh, *Apparitions and Shrines*, 3:98f.

[38] Ibid., 3:209ff.

[39] Ibid., 3:210.

[40] Ibid., 3:211.

[41] *Catholic Encyclopedia*, s.v. "St. Margaret Mary Alacoque."

[42] Walsh, *Apparitions and Shrines*, 3:213.

[43] Ibid., 3:213.

[44] Ibid., 3:125f.

[45] Ibid., 3:127.

[46] Ibid., 3:198.

[47] This account is given in Cyriel odhner Sigstedt, *The Swedenborg Epic: The Life and Works of Emmanuel Swedenborg* (New York: Bookman, 1952), 185f.

[48] Quoted by Rudolph L. Tafel, *Documents Concerning Swedenborg. Volume 1: The Life and Character of Emanuel Swedenborg* (London: Swedenborg Society, 1875), 35–36. Tafel's book is now available at http://www.heavenlydoctrines.org/Books%20and%20Monographs%5CDoc%20Vol%201.html (accessed January 31, 2014).

[49] Emanuel Swedenborg, *The Spiritual Diary of Emanuel Swedenborg Being the Record During Twenty Years of his Supernatural Experience*, trans. George Bush and John H. Smithson (Swedenborg Foundation, 1971), vol. 4, para. 4791m.

[50] *Spiritual Diary*, vol. 1, para. 651.

[51] Walsh, *Apparitions and Shrines*, 3:203f.

[52] Anne Catherine Emmerich, *The Dolorus Passion of Our Lord Jesus Christ* (Rockford, Ill.: Tan Books, 1983), 3.

[53] Walsh, *Apparitions and Shrines*, 3:203f.

[54] *Catholic Encyclopedia*, s.v. "Emmerich, Anne Catherine."

[55] Walsh, *Apparitions and Shrines*, 4:173. We might wonder why the wounds are said to have come from seven swords, rather than some other number, and why they are said to have come from swords, rather than some other sharp instrument. These facts are not explained, however.

[56] Walsh, *Apparitions and Shrines*, 4:174–5.

[57] Chester Huyssen and Lucille Huyssen, *Visions of Jesus* (Plainfield, N.J.: Logos International, 1977), 34. This book was reissued as *I Saw the Lord* (Tarrytown, N.Y.: Fleming H. Revell, 1992).

[58] Cyril J. Davey, *The Story of Sadhu Sundar Singh: The Saint of India* (Bromley UK: STL Books, 1980), 28.

[59] Ibid., 31–34. The vision is dated as having occurred on December 3, 1903.

[60] Walsh, *Apparitions and Shrines*, 4:214.

[61] Scott Sparrow, *I am With You Always: True Stories of Encounters with Jesus* (New York: Bantam Books, 1995).

[62] Further details about the experiences I researched can be found in my *Visions of Jesus: Direct Encounters from the New Testament to Today* (New York: Oxford University Press, 1997), which is a technical study of the phenomenon.

CHAPTER 4

VISIONS, DREAMS, AND TRANCES

The people whose experiences I will describe in these next chapters were discovered mostly through advertisements I placed in religious periodicals in Canada, the United States, Great Britain, and Australia. I also found a few through acquaintances who knew about my research interests. The advertisement asked those who had experienced what they took to be a "direct visual encounter with Jesus Christ" to write me a letter if they were interested in speaking with me.

Subsequent letters or telephone calls were usually enough to determine if the responder had experienced the kind of vision I wished to study, although the initial reluctance of some people to speak about such experiences sometimes prevented me from knowing enough about them until I conducted face-to-face interviews. I went all the way to Louisiana from my home in greater Vancouver, British Columbia, for example, only to discover that the woman who responded to one of my advertisements experienced a dream, not a vision. She would not tell me enough about her experience over the phone to indicate what had happened, so I made the long trip hoping I would find what I was looking for. I hoped in vain.

On another occasion, a person who had responded by letter had encountered a being the person took to be God, not Jesus. Again, this was not part of my research objectives. I undertook this study so I might learn as much as possible about a particular kind of experience that is evidently similar to the ones that helped establish the early Christian belief in the resurrection. For this reason, I questioned the volunteers closely about the details of their experiences.

I conducted most of the interviews between 1988 and 1993, and the accounts that follow are based on transcripts of conversations I had with the people involved. I do not know whether any of them would accept the designation "visionary," for most were quite mystified about having had such an experience, and none were in monastic life, although some were very active in their religious communities. None of them, moreover, seems to have attempted to produce their visionary experience or experiences deliberately, for example, by fasting, or depriving themselves of sleep or oxygen, or by ingesting hallucinogenic substances or foods. Most appeared to think of themselves as quite ordinary.

All of them were quite committed in their faith when I spoke to them, although a number indicated that this commitment had fluctuated in their lives, even after the visionary experiences. Quite a number of the people I interviewed live in my home province of British Columbia, which has only about four million people. The fact that I found as many as I did living near me suggests that the number of such experiences overall might be quite large.

The descriptions that follow do not generally include precise information on where these experiences took place, for that did not seem to be significant to the people involved. Many also have moved far from the places where their experiences took place and showed no evidence of attaching significance to the physical locations where the apparitions occurred (by erecting statues or shrines, for example). Visions of Mary, by contrast, have often been followed with many shrines to commemorate the experiences.

In the Temple of the Lord

Joy Kinsey was born in Oakland, California, and has lived in that area much of her life. One of her earliest memories is kneeling with her sister at her father's knee to say prayers just before bed. Joy and her sister went to the Presbyterian church near their home as children; but in 1947, when Joy was fourteen, she began to attend a Pentecostal Holiness church in Oakland, which is where her experience took place about ten years later. Prayer was a central feature in the life of her new church, and people would pray together for hours on end, sometimes all night long.

The informal nature of the services allowed people to come to the altar for prayer during the service, and this is what Joy did one evening, along with others, as the service was in progress. Her intention was "just to kneel and pray and just really totally surrender my will to God for whatever purpose." A minister came to pray with her, and when he touched the back of her head in a gesture of blessing, she fell backward and lost consciousness.

For three hours, Joy was unaware of anyone or anything around her. She had the sense of being in a temple that was surrounded by a courtyard. The temple had three domed parts to it, attached together so that they formed one continuous building. She began to walk through it, each part beautiful beyond description, but when she came to the threshold of the third part, she stopped, for she felt unworthy to enter. As she looked in, she saw Jesus sitting on a throne about fifteen feet away, but sitting sideways in relation to her and partially obscured by a lattice. He looked pleased at her having come so far, such as a parent might look upon seeing his or her child take its first steps. He appeared average in size, solid in appearance, and much as she pictured him.

Joy attempted to enter the third part of the temple, but he put out his hand in a gesture that indicated she could not. He told her from behind the lattice that she was not allowed to approach him. At hearing this, she fell to her knees and prostrated herself on the floor, which seemed to be made of marble or alabaster. It was so immaculate that she felt dirty and unworthy. She begged permission to approach closer, but he would not allow it, and instead instructed her to get up and go to a nearby window. She looked out of the window onto a landscape of fields and trees bent by the wind. He drew her attention in the ensuing conversation to a kite, which was barely flying because its tail was too long. He told her that her life was like the kite, burdened down by sins and encumbrances that impeded its flight. As she looked at the kite again its tail became caught in a tree, whereupon the one flying it yanked on the string and freed it to soar away, leaving half the tail in the tree. Jesus told her that her life could be like that kite. She left the window and fell on her knees again.

As she looked in front of her, she saw a goblet filled with wine. Jesus then said to her, "I will give you a new anointing. Drink the wine." As she obeyed, she could see him smiling at her. He was still seated, but now his hand was on the lattice in a parting gesture of blessing.

Joy regained consciousness and discovered that approximately three hours had elapsed since the vision had begun. She found the people around her were distressed because they smelled a strong aroma of sweet wine coming from her mouth. The smell filled the church, and she felt drunk. She was so wobbly that she could not stand on her own but needed two people to hold her up. When she tried to talk, she could not speak English but could speak only another language that she had not learned. Joy had never had an alcoholic drink in her life; moreover, her church practiced total abstinence, even refraining from the use of wine during communion services. Joy says the experience made her feel greatly loved by Jesus. Her life has been difficult at times, particularly because of the care required by her husband, who has Alzheimer's and Parkinson's diseases. But she has also sensed the sustaining presence of God. She lived in the Oakland area when I interviewed her.

Comment

This experience is the most dreamlike of all I came across, but the provocative effects Joy reported—the smell of wine that came from her and her inability to walk—suggest that the experience was more than a dream. I was not able to verify these aspects of her experience, however. Her parents, who would have been in the best position to verify her story had died long before I interviewed Joy.

Readers familiar with Acts of the Apostles will immediately notice the striking similarity between this experience and the one briefly described by Saint Luke in Acts 2 when the disciples of Jesus were suddenly able to speak languages they had not learned, leading bystanders to think the speakers were drunk. Luke does not say precisely what it was that gave observers the impression that the disciples were drunk; speaking languages they had had not learned does not suggest, by itself, that they were intoxicated. Perhaps they also exhibited another behavior, not mentioned by Luke, such as having difficulty standing up or walking. This feature could be described both by observers and those experiencing the intoxicating effect, and so transcends the private nature of most visions. Luke evidently knew some of the first disciples, and perhaps obtained his perspective on their experience firsthand, if he himself were not present at Pentecost.

Struggles with Darkness

Robin Wheeler had very little contact with the church or with Christians for the first thirty-eight years of his life. He occasionally went to a Catholic or an Anglican church when he was young, but he had no interest in religion until neighbors who were quite religious moved in and began speaking to him of their beliefs. His wife became a Christian as a result of the neighbors' influence. This annoyed him greatly, especially when she prayed openly for him.

One Saturday night several weeks after her conversion, Robin had what he described as a battle with an evil creature as he was trying to sleep. Its face resembled a human face without skin, and it frightened him. He tried in vain to fight off this creature. Just off to his right stood a man wearing a brown sackcloth robe with a sash around his waist. Robin never did see above the shoulders of this second figure, but he considers it to have been Jesus. Robin tried to tie up the creature with the sash from Jesus, and as he did so, Jesus disappeared. Again and again, he would struggle with the monster, and each time Jesus would appear long enough for Robin to grab the sash and then disappear.

Robin's wife was with him while this struggle was taking place. She told me that he levitated for long periods of time that coincided with the struggles, and seemed to go in and out of consciousness. She said Robin floated in midair in a horizontal position about a foot above the bed, that his body was in a perfectly rigid position, and that all the veins in his body were bulging. His head was bent so far back, she said, that she thought it would break. Although she did not see the figures that appeared to him, she could ask him what was happening, and he would describe the events taking place. She estimated that the various struggles occurred over a six-hour period, but he had no sense of the passing of time.

When a fight sequence came to an end, his body would drop back onto the bed, and he would relax until a new struggle began. But Robin was not aware of his levitation. During the fights, he could see his wife as well as these two other beings, and they seemed as real as ordinary persons. The place he seemed to be in did not fit with the physical description of the bedroom, however. Jesus would appear with Roman sandals, and he entered the scene with his feet first, as though he descended from above. The struggles finally ended when Robin found that his efforts to tie up the monster did not succeed, and he requested help from Jesus, who bound the monster for him.

Robin considered this to be symbolic of his own inability to restrain the powers of evil that tried to envelop him. The next day Robin decided to become a Christian. This event took place in British Columbia in 1984.

Comment

This is one of the few experiences I heard about that involved a struggle with forces considered to be diabolical. Robin's wife clearly understood the levitation she witnessed as something which anyone could have seen, if they had been present, although no one else was there to see it. Their children and pets were elsewhere in the house and slept through the bizarre events, even though Robin shouted all night long.

Robin and his wife said they interpreted this deep sleep as indicative of unseen forces that were controlling the events of that night. Robin's wife expressed no surprise at the fact that he had levitated, for she said she had witnessed levitation of other people on several occasions. Both said they had been involved in occult practices earlier in their lives.

Robin's experience was interesting because both his and his wife's accounts were important in making it complete. He was in a state that would generally be described as a trance, although this description does not provide much additional insight to those of us who have not been in trances. The experience is interesting because the levitation indicates that some power or agent was active—these kinds of phenomena are strongly suggestive of an order of reality that acts upon the ordinary space-time-causal world that we normally experience.

"I Died for You and I Am God"

Marian Hathaway was brought up in Swansea, Wales, as an atheist by parents who were atheists. She said she was really a third-generation atheist, for her paternal grandfather had also been an atheist. She wanted to believe in God when she was young but could not find any reason to do so.

When she was seventeen, she had a dream in which a man with dark bushy hair came toward her with his arms open, asking her to love him. She said she knew it was Jesus, even though she did not know much about him. She had heard a story about Jesus born in a manger, who grew up to be a good man, but that was the extent of her knowledge. Her education in a state school included prayers and religious instruction, but these meant nothing to her.

Marian married soon after secondary school and had children, but she was not happy. She gradually became so depressed that it interfered with her ability to work, and she began to contemplate suicide. In her desperation, she prayed to God for help. She soon began to sleep better, which she attributed to her prayer. She then went to hospital for a short stint in order to rid her body of toxins that had accumulated from the medications she had been taking. She began to feel better, and she wondered if her prayer for help had worked.

Several days after returning home, Marian received a visit from a young couple who belonged to the Jehovah's Witnesses. Marian was very receptive to the things they said, and soon they were visiting her four times a week to instruct her. But the position of the Jehovah's Witnesses on blood transfusions—that they violate Scripture—was a point of contention with her mother, who encouraged an old family friend from a Baptist church to visit Marian. Marian now heard a different point of view on a variety of subjects.

For the next seven months, she studied both points of view. She asked God to show her the truth, particularly about the divinity of Jesus, but felt desperate about ever finding it because of her own sense of unworthiness. In Easter week of 1969, as she was riding the bus home from one of these instructional meetings, she heard the words inside her, "I died for you, and I love you just the way you are, with all your sin." Then she heard the words, "I am God." At this she burst into tears of joy. The bus driver asked her if she was all right as she left the bus, and she assured him she was. The question that remained, as a result of this experience, was which among the many conventional Christian churches she should attend.

Marian decided to attend the Baptist church with the old family friend. She worried greatly about being at the service, however, wondering if it was the right thing to do. She was seated in the balcony of the church, and as she looked toward the large pipe organ she saw shimmering blue and gold colors in front of it. The images reminded her of the jumpy pictures of the earliest silent movies. They gradually became clearer until she found herself looking at a big face with beautiful golden hair and a golden beard. The face was so large it filled the front of the church—some twenty feet high. She thought it must be Jesus, but she was puzzled by the fact that he neither looked Jewish nor resembled the image of the person that appeared in her dream when she was seventeen.

She saw him looking at the congregation, with a smile and an expression of love for the people. Then she saw his arms, draped in white, move in an embrace of everyone present at the service. They were large enough to take in several rows at once. To describe his action, Marian used a Welsh word meaning to cuddle, to comfort, or to love by touching someone. He loved everyone there, including her. She kissed his cheek in response, and physically felt his warmth, although not the feel of his skin.

Because Marian did not know if this experience was real or imaginary, she closed her eyes, but she could still see him with her eyes closed. When she opened them a moment later, he was still there. This went on for some time, and Marian felt assured that she had come to the right place. This experience filled her with such awe, she could hardly believe it had taken place. When she went home that day she prayed, asking God whether it was really Jesus that had appeared to her, and if it was, why he appeared with only his face and arms.

She reached for her Bible, which was still quite new to her, and opened it at random to a passage in Ephesians 1 that speaks of Jesus being the head of the church, and the church being his body. Everything fell into place for her at that moment, and Christian beliefs about him and his death became clear. This experience took place in Swansea in 1969 when Marian was thirty years old.

Comment

This was one of the few experiences in which I interviewed the person in the exact place where the vision took place. It was also one of the few in which the figure that appeared was described as much larger than life-size and was the only case in which having one's eyes open or closed made no difference. Perhaps Augustine would have classified it as an imaginative vision rather than a corporeal one, because a question could be raised about whether Marian actually used her eyes in seeing what she saw. But she certainly gave the impression in the interview of having initially used her eyes, for she convincingly showed me exactly where the shimmering effect was first seen, where she was seated, how high the image appeared, and the location of the organ against which the image was seen.

The two experiences previously described are clearly trancelike in character, whereas this one is less so, since Marian was awake. Yet it has strange qualities, for it made no difference if her eyes were open or shut. Her experience illustrates the difficulty in classifying visions in precise categories.

The experiences of Robin and Marian, as well as some others, suggest that a strong religious background is not necessary to experience a vision. In this respect, these and other people I interviewed differ from the saints of Christian history whose visions have shaped attitudes about the conditions under which visions of Jesus occur.

The Presence

John Vasse was brought up in a devout Catholic home in Fairfield, Connecticut, where he attended church regularly as a child, and was educated at a Jesuit high school. But something he did not divulge happened halfway through high school that made him turn his back on God and the church. For the next twenty-six years or so, he was filled with loathing and contempt for God. He would go into churches to scream at and curse the figure on the crucifix, daring Jesus to come off the cross so he could physically abuse him.

Meanwhile, he attended college, graduated with a degree in engineering, married, and entered the U. S. Air Force. Although he held down a number of good engineering jobs, his life revolved around going to bars and consuming alcohol. He drank so much that by the time he was forty he had damaged his liver and suffered an apparent heart attack. His drinking also affected his marriage, and he felt as though his life had reached bottom when he got word he was being transferred to Saint Louis, where his wife was unwilling to move.

At this point, a friend who had recently become a Christian suggested to John that he should follow his example. John decided there was nothing to lose by praying, and so he prayed, apologizing to God for the way he had behaved for most of his life. He took the transfer to Saint Louis, and after about six months, his wife decided to join him there. On Christmas Day that year, 1984, an experience changed his life.

John and his wife tried to go to church on Christmas Eve, but ice had made the highways treacherous. The roads had not improved much by morning, so they stayed in their apartment and ate a late breakfast. As John sat at the table after breakfast, reading the editorial pages of the local paper, he had the uncomfortable and peculiar feeling that someone was standing behind him. He knew that no one was there, but nevertheless felt a "presence" who wanted "entry." John felt he had the choice of excluding this unidentified presence or inviting it in, and made a split-second decision: "OK, sure, come on in." He was immediately flooded with a weight of despondency or heaviness. But it did not seem to be his own despondency that he was feeling, but that of the presence he had invited in. John began to weep uncontrollably because of it, and went to the bathroom so he would not be seen crying.

He locked the door and stood before the mirror as this weight became heavier and heavier. As he stood there, he realized the presence he was feeling was Jesus. As he reflected on his contemptuous attitude in the past, John was filled with enormous guilt and shame. He fell to his knees and began to weep uncontrollably again, wetting his clothes, his shoes, and the bathroom floor with his tears. He sobbed, "Please forgive me, please forgive me." He wanted to crawl into the tub, pull the shade around himself and hide from this presence, but he was unable to move.

As he continued to beg forgiveness, he felt as though two plugs at the bottom of his feet popped out, and all the shame and guilt in him drained away as water would drain out of a bathtub. He was still immobilized, but the feelings of guilt and shame disappeared. The presence gradually faded, and he returned to the kitchen table, but could not talk to his wife about what had just happened. He anticipated that something else was going to happen, and in less than a minute, the presence he had felt before was back.

John did not want to fall onto the floor of the kitchen, so he walked toward the couch in the living room. Halfway there, he collapsed. Again the weight crushed him, but this time it did not last. It lifted, and the whole room was flooded with light, but not from any apparent natural source. He says the wall of the living room in front of him was as bright as the sun, but he could look into it without hurting his eyes. In the center was an area not illuminated quite as intensely as the rest, and here he could see the outline of a head, neck, and shoulders, like a cameo. He was instinctively certain that this was Jesus, from whom came an overpowering sense of love and compassion that extended to John and then returned back as though in circular motion.

The intensity of the light surrounding the figure obliterated facial features and other details. Ecstatic joy replaced John's earlier sense of anguish and despondency. As the experience came to an end, Jesus raised his hands in an inviting gesture. The whole experience lasted about thirty minutes—John happened to look at his watch before and after—and he had no control from the moment he made the decision to let the presence in. John was not sure if his eyes were open during the visual part of the experience, and he is uncertain about whether the figure appeared on the wall in front of him or was present only in his own visual space. His wife was in the apartment at the time but saw nothing.

When I interviewed John, he was working as a computer systems analyst and also with an organization that seeks to develop lay leadership in the church.

Comment

The visual elements of this experience were clearly secondary to the emotional effects of it, and the difficulty that John had in determining whether the figure that appeared was present only in his visual space or might have been visibly present, as this is normally understood, leads me to classify it with the trance cases. Though this was not the only experience in which a presence was strongly felt, it is a striking example. Andrew Mackenzie contends that presences should be included as apparitions, "although the experience is not externalized."[1] He remarks that figures can sometimes be described in detail even though they are not seen, and he rejects the common view that things that are only "felt" and not seen are experientially inferior.[2] John's experience seems to have hovered between an altered state of consciousness and ordinary perception.

Can These Experiences be Explained?

"Easy explanations" are often offered for the visions that people see. For example, visions are sometimes explained by saying that the people who had them ate too much spicy food the night before, or that they were looking for such experiences, or that they were reacting to the stress in their lives. I refer to such "explanations" as easy ones because those who offer them often do so without checking out the facts.

Take the first of these explanations, for example. We might legitimately ask how often eating spicy food results in a vision, and how spicy the food has to be in order to produce a vision! We might wonder whether mild Mexican taco sauce counts as spicy food and puzzle over the fact that spicy food, if we can decide what that is, does not always produce visions. These legitimate queries show that an explanation that refers to the effects of spicy food has not been well thought out. Similar critical questions could be directed toward the other "easy explanations" mentioned above.

A more serious explanation for both dreams and visions has been advanced by psychiatrists and brain researchers. Psychiatrist Louis West suggests in his article "A Clinical and Theoretical Overview of Hallucinatory Phenomena" that visions could result from little-understood mechanisms in the brain whereby previous perceptual experiences are combined and transformed in our memory and then released into the conscious life of certain individuals, for reasons poorly understood at present. Something like this seems to occur in dreams, for in dreams we often relive previous experiences in a disjointed way, with parts of one experience awkwardly joined with parts of another. Most of us never experience the release of ineptly joined memories during our conscious lives; we only experience this during sleep, and call the experience a dream. But a small number of people, according to this theory, which is formally known as the *perceptual release theory*, have a dreamlike experience while awake.

This explanation is still somewhat sketchy, for no definite mechanism is identified that causes visions to be experienced by some people but not by others. Moreover, it cannot adequately account for religious visions among those who have no religious background. Whether the neural sciences will be able to explain visions adequately is not yet clear. We can expect that science will discover that all perceptual experience, including visions, involves the complex brain functions found in humans, but this by itself does not establish that no source outside the experiencer is not involved.

Although the question of whether spiritual realities cause certain vision experiences remains open, the trancelike experiences described in this chapter are not the most plausible grounds for defending such a position.

Notes

[1] Andrew Mackenzie, *Apparitions and Ghosts: A Modern Study* (London: Arthur Barker, 1971), 7.

[2] Ibid., 273.

CHAPTER 5

HEAVEN ON EARTH

Some visions give the impression that heaven has come to earth for a moment, while others suggest that the visionary has had a glimpse of heaven. Talk about heaven is often symbolic, rather than literal, but the unusual perceptions that take place during visions often give those who experience them the sense that heaven is real.

The "location" of heaven is a problem for many people. Tradition says it lies above a flat earth, but this makes no sense to anyone familiar with physics and astronomy. Science teaches us that the direction of places in the universe is relative to the location of the observer. But science also teaches us that our senses are capable of perceiving only a minuscule portion of the actual universe. Could another "world" somehow be superimposed on our familiar world, capable of being glimpsed momentarily by individuals singled out to bear witness to its reality? No easy answer exists for that question.

Some explanation must be given for the strange perceptions reported in this book and elsewhere. Too many cases have been put forward simply to dismiss them all as fiction, produced by overactive imaginations.

Where Are the Dead?

Marian Galiffe was devastated by the death of her son, Joe. A week after his funeral she began to lock herself in his room for long periods of time, just to lie on his bed and be alone with his childhood toys and other mementos of him. Joe was killed in a traffic accident at the age of eighteen, the only fatality in a car carrying four other teenagers. He had been an extraordinarily caring child, and so his death left a great void in the lives of Marian and her husband. One afternoon as she lay on his bed, she began to express her anger toward God, demanding an answer to the question of how he could have caused or allowed Joe to die. She felt betrayed by God, for she had been devoted to God and had tried to obey him. She fell asleep after this outburst and awakened around nine o'clock that evening. She felt as though someone had awakened her, but no one else was around.

As Marian sat up, she felt as though she was commanded to go downstairs and gather her family for prayer and a reading from the Bible. She went downstairs to join her family in the living room, but didn't quite know how to convey the command, thinking that her family would think her mad if she spoke about it. She finally told her husband that she wanted to read the Bible and pray, and he consented. As she opened the Bible to a passage in the Gospel of Saint John, she sensed a command to stand up.

Marian, her husband, and their children stood as she read, and then joined hands to pray. At that moment, the back door flew open from what seemed to be a gust of wind, and a breeze moved through the room. The atmosphere of the room suddenly changed. A painful sensation creased Marian's chest, and she wondered aloud how much more pain she would have to bear. Then a light brighter than anything she had ever seen exploded upon her and filled the room.

The light gradually faded, and a man dressed in white came into view. It was Jesus. He appeared to be transparent rather than solid, and his long hair caught her attention. She first saw his profile, and then he turned to her, stretched out his hand, and commanded her (so it seemed) to look down the length of his arm. As she did so, his body disappeared from view until she could see only his hand. From the end of his hand, a hill covered with green grass began to form. As her attention was directed toward the hill, she saw Joe running toward her with three other children. Joe was wearing his favorite checkered shirt, blue jeans and jacket, and the belt with the big brass Harley Davidson buckle. She kept saying, "Look at our Joe. Our Joe's coming."

But the command came to her, "Look past Joe. Haven't you forgotten them? They are with me." Then she realized who the smaller children were. One was her child from a pregnancy that had been terminated because of fibroids in her womb, and the two other children were twins she later lost because of the effect of the terminated pregnancy. The twins would have been fourteen if they had lived, and the other child sixteen, and the three children who appeared with Joe seemed to be of these ages. Marian's sorrow turned to joy at the realization of who the children were. In response to encouragement from Joe, she began to sing in praise to God.

Marian's husband told me that he did not see any of the things that she reported, but he observed that she was "in an extraordinary ecstasy" as these events unfolded. Her attitude toward the death of her son changed after that, and she now felt like saying to everyone she knew, "Joe is alive, do you realize? I know now that we're all going to meet him." When they went through Joe's room sometime later, she found the clothes she had seen him wear in the vision. Marian lived in London, England, when I interviewed her in 1993, working as a homemaker and dressmaker. The experience had taken place two years earlier.

Comment

Marian's story is interesting because it suggests that even the lives of those who have never been born continue after death. Traditional Christianity teaches that every human being survives death in some mysterious form. The usual way of describing this is to say that the soul is immortal, but unborn children are not always included among the beings with souls. Marian's experience suggests otherwise. She seems to have seen into "the beyond" where the deceased live, grow up, and are reunited with members of their earthly family.

The claim that infants are cared for in heaven was curiously defended by a visionary from the nineteenth century. Marietta Davis is said to have been in trance for nine days, from which she could not be awakened. In *Scenes Beyond the Grave*, she told of seeing angels in various ranks receiving and then caring for children.[1]

"If I Could Only Touch You"

Eve Zelle was brought up in the eastern United States with a variety of Christian influences. She was born into a Greek Orthodox family and raised in that church, but sometime in her youth her family adopted the beliefs of the Jehovah's Witnesses. By fourteen she had abandoned most of her religious ideas, apart from believing that God exists. She occasionally went to a Catholic church with some of her friends and attended a Catholic college because it was near her home.

She majored in mathematics with a minor in Catholic philosophy, and became a teacher. After she married and had children, she took them to church, and at some point in her thirties, she finally felt comfortable calling herself a Christian. She began to go to various churches, both Protestant and Catholic, as well as to Bible studies, in order to learn whatever she could about being a Christian. Eve's first experience took place in 1987 or 1988, when she was about forty-six years old. By this time she was single, responsible for two teenage daughters, and unemployed.

Eve was desperate about her situation. Not only had she been without work for a long time, but her oldest daughter was giving her a hard time. Eve began to feel that God was not aware of her need, and she wondered if he was real, or if she was only fooling herself about his existence. She remembers extending her hand in a moment of desperate prayer and saying to God, "If I could only touch you, if I could only touch your hand." She opened her eyes, and was startled to see Jesus in front of her. "He was on his knees holding both my hands with the most compassionate, warm eyes that I had ever seen, with strength behind them," Eve says.

The look on his face extended warmth and compassion toward her and let her know he understood her desperation. He had large brown eyes and looked Jewish to her, but she could not recall anything else about his appearance, although she thought he had a short beard. He appeared to be normal in size, although an assessment of this was difficult because he was kneeling. Her impression was that he was wearing white clothing, but she could not say whether it was the kind of robe traditionally associated with him. Though the experience was comforting and reassuring, it also scared her, and she ran from the room.

An odd feature of the experience was that she was kneeling, facing her bed, when it took place. Eve's words were: "He was where the bed would have been, and there was nothing else." She is at a loss to explain how the perceptual sense of the bed could disappear and how she could see Jesus in its place, for her eyes were open.

Eve had a second experience some two years later, again in response to prayer. Eve describes herself as very pro-life, and she was devastated to learn that a close friend had chosen to have an abortion. She walked "screaming angry" into her bedroom to pray about this, but before her knees hit the floor she saw Jesus standing and holding a baby. He held it in such a way that the baby seemed part of him. She could see the head of a child, but the rest of the child blended in with him. She got the sense that he had received the aborted child, and that he was not bringing condemnation on its mother. He gave the sense of taking care of his own children.

Jesus appeared to be about six feet tall and was standing some eight feet away, clothed in robes that Eve described as priestly in color, perhaps blue trimmed with gold. Although Eve was in her bedroom when this took place, all she could see was Jesus. It seemed as though all the normal furniture in the room had disappeared, much as in the first experience in which her bed disappeared. Both of the experiences gave her a sense that God is deeply concerned about her life.

Comment

Eve's second experience corroborates Marian Gallife's impression that Christ loves and receives even the children who are never born. This possibility can be a source of comfort for those whose little children died either before being born or soon afterward. It also provides solace for those who have had abortions and have come to regret their decisions.

Eve's experiences also raises interesting questions about the sense of spatial location in visionary experiences. How could the bed disappear from view, and Jesus take its place? Here is an educated woman who had the sense of never having left her room but finding that the room's furniture had suddenly disappeared. In my research I encountered several people who reported experiences in which they seemed to leave their bodies, for they had a definite sense of moving from one location to another. Eve reported nothing of the kind—her experience seemed to take place right in the room she knew herself to be in. Heaven seemed to visit her, and to obliterate the things of earth for a moment.

This kind of vision is difficult to understand. Even Christians who accept the reality of Jesus and heaven must admit that they have no simple explanation for it. Experiences of this kind are in conflict with the usual categories used in explanations, even by Christians, and also challenge our usual conception of space.

The Case of the Hardened Criminal

Ernie Hollands was born in 1930 in the slums of Halifax, Nova Scotia, to what would now be called a dysfunctional family. Alcoholism, as well as physical and emotional abuse, characterizes memories of his earliest years, and he has no memory of having been loved or embraced. His "private education" began at eight when his mother took him shopping and taught him how to steal. By the time he was ten he was quite expert at it, but Ernie was caught and sent to reform school. The challenge of escape was appealing, and thus began a cycle of crime, arrest, detention, and escape. Numerous Canadian and American prisons were "home" for Ernie during the next twenty-five years or so. The events that changed his life took place when he was incarcerated at Millhaven Penitentiary in Bath, Ontario.

During his prison term in Millhaven, Ernie developed a successful business selling hand-tied fishing flies. One of his business contacts, Grant Bailey from Pembroke, Ontario, urged Ernie to read the Bible and become a Christian. Ernie's initial response was contempt, but the warmth of friendship extended to him by Grant made him reconsider, and so Ernie began to read and reread the Bible.

On March 12, 1975, at two o'clock in the morning, Ernie awoke with the sense that he should confess his sins to God. He wept as he knelt down by his bed to pray, and felt that his past had been forgiven. When he stood up, his vision, as he calls it, began. He turned to look at the door of his cell, for no particular reason, but what he saw was no longer his cell but the room of a house with a door on the right side of it, positioned where the cell door was located. This door opened up, and Jesus walked through it toward Ernie, stood in front of him, touched him on his left shoulder (which he felt) and said three things.

He first said, "I'm so glad you didn't kill that police officer," and then he smiled. Ernie understood this to be a reference to the crime he had committed before being sent to Millhaven. In the course of a robbery of a supermarket in Hollywood, California, he had struggled with a policeman for control of a stolen gun, and in the tussle he accidentally shot the policeman in the leg. Ernie then gave himself up, hoping that the policeman would perhaps shoot him and put him out of misery. Instead, he found himself incarcerated in Los Angeles until he was released to the Canadian authorities for crimes committed in Canada. Then Jesus said, "Your slate is now wiped clean," and here he moved his hands in a way that suggested that something was being erased. The third thing Jesus said was, "Now you can start all over again," making a semicircular motion with his arms, to suggest that Ernie was being sent to live a new life. Then Jesus disappeared.

Jesus appeared to Ernie much as he is traditionally portrayed, wearing white, and of medium height. Ernie was not able to be more precise about any other physical details, however. He describes the three statements Jesus made as sounding as though they came from inside himself, and he was not aware of Jesus' lips moving as these things were uttered. He describes the voice as though it was thunder coming from inside of himself. Ernie's story was reported by the

Ottawa press and has become widely known through his own telling of it in person and through a book.[2] In 1983 he opened Hebron Farm near London, Ontario, as a Christian home for ex-offenders, dedicated to helping them obtain employment and readjust to society.

Comment

The messages given to Ernie were clearly the dominant features of this vision. Again we find a strange spatial feature, as though heaven had become superimposed upon the prison cell that was home to Ernie. But this is almost incidental to this life-changing event. Ernie's book does not describe the fact that his prison cell was transformed, and he mentioned to me in the interview that he did not usually share this part of his experience with audiences. No doubt he wanted to leave them with a positive message, not with questions about the unpredictable character of visions.

However, we should give some thought to this curious feature of many visions. These experiences are unquestionably of great significance for many—I want to say "all," but I recognize the possibility that I failed to encounter those who did not find the experience significant—and might actually be heavenly encounters. Is it possible that when God reveals something about the domain he inhabits, he also introduces something that will puzzle us? As he reveals, does he also conceal?

Just Too Much TV?

Jim Link was watching a movie on television one evening in his home in Ontario when the screen suddenly became invisible. The first thought that occurred to him, which he knew to be absurd, was that maybe he had watched so much television that he had become blind! He next realized that he was unable to hear the television set, and he thought, "Have I been watching so much TV that it is affecting my vision and my hearing?" He stood up to look out of the window next to him just to make sure his eyesight was still intact, but he couldn't see the walls. It seemed as though he was enclosed in a curtain, but he couldn't really see a curtain.

A human figure then came into view at the end of the room, starting with an outline that became clearer and clearer, until he could see someone wearing long robes and sandals. He wondered, "What's going on here? Who is this? What is this?" The figure turned to face Jim, extended an arm, and beckoned Jim three times to come to him. Jim immediately thought to himself, "That is Jesus!" and the lines came to him from the New Testament, "Come to me all you who are weak and heavy laden, and I will give you rest." He thought to himself, "It's real, then; it's real. I have to ask for forgiveness and repent and receive him." At that instant everything in the room returned to normal, and he decided to become a Christian.

The figure that Jim saw was of average height and seemed to be situated about fifteen to eighteen feet away. The robe the figure wore was a dark blue or a purplish blue; Jim was not sure which. What impressed Jim most was the royalty of the appearance and the way the figure welcomed him. The figure wore a hood that hid his face, so Jim could not report anything about facial features.

Jim had been wondering about the meaning of life, what his purpose in life was, and whether he was just on earth to work and maintain a home and watch television! He had been attending church with his wife, just to please her, but having this experience at age twenty-seven changed his outlook on life.

Jim had another experience in 1977, some fifteen years later, one evening after a Bible study in the home of his brother-in-law. He was sitting at the kitchen table, just having had coffee and something to eat. He tried to get up but discovered he was unable to move. He turned to tell his brother-in-law sitting several feet away about this sudden inability to move, but he could not see him. All he could see was the face of one he took to be Jesus "from sort of three-quarters of the way down his forehead to just below his chin, just as clear as you're sitting there right now," Jim said.

The radiant or glowing figure seen as Jesus had a beard and brown shoulder-length hair, and looked like the popular images of Jesus in pictures. Just to convince himself that he was seeing something genuine, Jim looked away and then looked back again to see if the figure still was there, and he was able to do this several times. Jim was the only one in the room who could see the figure, however.

As he got up a few minutes later to go home, he was flattened by a force that pinned him to the floor. For about three hours he was interrogated by this being about what he valued most—his job, his family, his wife, his possessions, and so on. The others in the group watched in awe but said nothing. They heard Jim's responses, but not the questions that were put to him. His brother-in-law wanted to come over to him to pray with him, Jim reported, but could not do so—it was as if an invisible line had been drawn across the floor that he could not cross. Jim describes the second experience as having confirmed his decision earlier in life to be a Christian. Jim does some oil painting as a hobby, and in the front entrance of his home hangs a painting of a biblical scene in which he tried to capture the likeness as he had seen it. It resembles traditional views of Jesus' appearance.

When I interviewed Jim in 1988, he worked in Toronto as a supply manager for an electrical company, and also did some lay preaching. Since that time he has gone into pastoral work.

Comment

Few experiences that I encountered in my research portray Jesus in his awesome role as judge. His work as loving Savior is most commonly reported, which is also true of the accounts that have come down to us in history. Jim's experience suggests that visions of Jesus are capable of revealing various aspects of Christ's person and offices, including one that is capable of instilling respect and even a certain amount of fear.

The Face of Compassion

Kris Nelson's experience took place in the context of a long, drawn-out illness. She went into the hospital to have a hysterectomy, thinking she would recuperate in six weeks or so, but the operation was followed by complications, including internal bleeding, thrombosis, and blood infections. Two more operations were required before her health improved, and she found herself incapacitated for six months rather than six weeks.

Just before her last operation, the doctor came to her home to assess her condition. When she heard that another operation would be required, she was devastated, for she knew that her husband and her children needed her at home. As she lay in bed feeling very sad, a sense of peace unexpectedly came over her. She glanced over to the corner of the room, for no apparent reason, and saw the face of Jesus. She describes his face as having been the mirror image of how she had felt. The hurt and sadness were on his face, and tears streamed down his face, as though he was identifying with her sadness. When Kris saw him she felt that all would be well in just a little while.

Kris saw only his face, which appeared eight to ten feet away and looked very lifelike in the well-lit room. She described his appearance as quite ordinary, and not quite like any portrayals she had seen. His hair was fairly long and brown, and Kris was not sure whether he had a beard. It was his eyes that caught her attention, for they seemed to show that he knew her heart and was sympathetic. Some radiance shone around his head, but not so much as to obscure the image itself. Kris does not know how she made the identification of the person as Jesus, but did not hesitate in doing so. The only medication she was on at the time was an antibiotic.

Kris was a secretary as well as a homemaker when I interviewed her in 1993, and had lived in Melbourne, Australia, all her life. Her experience had taken place during the previous year.

Comment

This experience is peculiar because it involved the visual perception of only a face. It is not really like the trance experiences described earlier, nor the cases to follow in which the physical environment changed, nor those in which the whole figure was "superimposed," so to speak, upon the normal environment. Again, the emotional aspects, or, to speak more precisely, the *affective* aspects of the experience, not the perceptual aspects, were uppermost for Kris.

The Face in the Blinds

Rose was brought up in a Greek Orthodox home, and because her husband was from another denominational background, they could not agree about religious matters, including where they should go to church. So they didn't attend anywhere.

Rose's first vision occurred about 1963. She was not sure of the date, because the significance of it did not really dawn on her until some time afterward. She was lying in bed one morning, wide awake, when the venetian blinds opened up and the head of Jesus appeared. Only his bearded head was visible, but for Rose it was the most beautiful face with the bluest of eyes. The first thought that came to her was that she should pray. She thought it would be selfish to pray for herself, so she prayed, "Would you save thy people?" As she said this, tears came into his eyes and rolled down his cheeks. Then he vanished.

She woke her husband to tell him what had happened. The venetian blinds had been closed before this incident took place, but when the head of Jesus appeared, they mysteriously opened. The head appeared solid, for Rose could see the blinds on either side but not the blinds behind the head. She estimates that he was some six to eight feet away, and that his size looked normal for that distance. The experience made her feel elated, as though she were floating. She could hardly contain the news. After this she began to attend church periodically, but no particularly significant change in her religious life occurred as a result of it.

Rose's second vision took place in Palm Springs, California, on October 29, 1988, early in the morning. Again she was lying in her bed, and again Jesus appeared about six to eight feet away, but on this occasion she saw his whole form standing in the doorway of the bedroom. He wore a robe, off-white in color, loosely tied up by a cord. Again she was attracted to his face, especially his eyes. He had brown curly hair, and a beard to match his hair, and again his eyes were blue. This point puzzled her then and still does, for she doesn't think that a Jewish person would have blue eyes. His facial expression was pleasant, but he was not smiling. He stood there for some seconds and then disappeared. The experience seemed as real to Rose as if a normal person had stood there. No message was communicated on this occasion, and Rose believed its purpose was simply to let her know that he exists.

Explaining Diversity

Visions of Jesus are often dismissed as insignificant or perhaps are thought to be significant only for those who experience them. This and other stereotypes of what visions are like are entertained, I believe, because of insufficient information about the actual nature of visions or apparitions, or whatever these phenomena should be called. However, the accounts given up to this point show that these experiences are not like the stereotype just described. Their variety suggests that an adequate explanation for them will not be easy to discover.

Naturalists believe that everything can be explained using the concepts derived from ordinary experience, psychology, or neurophysiology, and that supernatural explanations are not needed at all. However, naturalistic explanations for the varied kinds of events reported in these chapters are not available. Insisting that such explanations will be forthcoming is an article of faith, and not much more reliable than a similar insistence from a Christian that supernatural explanations can be given. Appeals to both natural and supernatural causes are incomplete at present and might always be so.

The reader might have noticed that very few of the visions that have come to us in the "devotional" literature of the Christian faith— whether Catholic, Orthodox, or Protestant—come with many details about what was actually experienced, including how Jesus looked: the color of his eyes, the style of his hair, what he was wearing, whether other perceptual features (such as touch) were also experienced, and so on. These are the details, however, that determine whether naturalistic explanations might be adequate to explain them all, or whether features are present that suggest the existence of "another" world, or a realm beyond the ordinary one.

Notes

[1] Huyssen and Huyssen, *Visions of Jesus*, 28f.

[2] Ernie Hollands, *Hooked* (Toronto: Mainroads, 1983). Ernie passed away in October, 1996.

CHAPTER 6

PRIVATE EXPERIENCES

Quite a number of people I interviewed experienced their visions when they were alone, so we cannot readily predict what someone else might have experienced if they had been present. A sizable number took place in a public setting, but other people who were present were evidently unable to see what the visionary did. Such experiences undoubtedly give the impression that visions are always subjective experiences. However, we must not be too quick to draw this conclusion, as can be seen from some incidents in the following chapter.

In this chapter, the cases I present were experienced by individuals on their own, and this is the feature they have in common. But even this subgroup of cases exhibit a surprising amount of variety.

A Few Moments Frozen in Time

Ethel Chilvers had a visionary experience in her small apartment in Toronto when she was ninety-one years old. She was in the kitchen washing dishes, and when she looked in the direction of a table some six to eight feet away, she saw the figure of Jesus in profile above the table. He was not walking or moving, but seemed to be in midstride, facing the direction of the city center. She said he appeared much as he does in children's picture books, with brown shoulder-length hair, beard, white skin, and of average size. He wore a cape or cloak similar to that which she had seen worn by a man from Afghanistan who lived in her apartment block.

Jesus did not move at all, and his appearance was like that of a statue, but a solid, living statue. Ethel said, "It was just as though a man stood there. It could have been you." He did not appear happy or pleased but seemed to her as though he wanted to "execute judgment on somebody somewhere or do something. I felt like he was capable of destroying the whole world. I had the sense that he had that much power, that he could stop it [the world] if he wanted to, but he was restrained from doing it." He somehow communicated all this without saying a word. She later reflected on the sense of power that he seemed to have, and felt that what was restraining him was his love for humanity.

Ethel had immigrated to Canada from England with her parents when she was six years old. She trained as a nurse in Port Simpson Hospital and Vancouver General Hospital from 1918 to 1921 and practiced nursing for about sixty years. She was brought up in the Methodist Church and attended a variety of churches during her lifetime. I spoke to her when she was ninety-three, and although her health was beginning to fail, she was lively in conversation and continued to read and keep up correspondence with friends.

Comment

Most of the people who talked with me said their experiences carried great personal significance and were often related to some difficult or tragic feature of their lives. Ethel's experience was different, inasmuch as it did not carry any significant personal message for her. The experience made her regret not having pursued more conscientiously plans she had when she was much younger to work as a missionary nurse in China, but the experience was not interpreted by her in a distinctly personal way. The fact that the figure showed no movement at all and was seen only in profile made this experience unusual.

Drawn into Another World

Deby Stamm-Loya moved home just before Christmas 1972 to live with her parents in Tucson, Arizona, after her marriage failed. She watched a movie one evening with her parents that awakened a desire to know God better. She went to her bed and began to think about life and the desire the movie had evoked. She lay on her back for some time with her eyes closed, thinking about these things, and when she opened them some minutes later a man she instantly identified as Jesus stood at the end of her bed some five or six feet away.

His arms were stretched out as though he was reaching for her. He stood there for a moment, appearing much as he does in traditional portrayals of him and much like any normal person would appear. Then he began to change. A radiance enveloped him—pure white light that gradually increased in intensity. As this radiance intensified, it extended farther and farther beyond him, so that it finally consisted of a pure white light nearest to him and various shades of yellow, orange, and amber beyond the whiteness. As this transformation took place, Deby became conscious of being drawn into the immense universe of which he seemed a part, and she had the sense of being in a place far removed from her parents' home. Then she lost natural consciousness and became aware only of his voice and the things he said to her.

In reflecting back on the experience, Deby said the spoken message had the greatest significance for her. He told her that he had everything in the universe under control, including her life, and that he had many things to teach her. He said he loved her and that she should keep her attention fixed on him. How long this experience lasted she did not know, for when she regained natural consciousness she was in her bed, and it was morning. She firmly believed she had not fallen asleep at the time the vision (her term) began, because she did not typically fall asleep lying on her back. Moreover, the bedroom door was open to the adjacent room where her parents were sitting, and she saw the figure standing at the end of her bed against the backdrop of that room.

Deby had a difficult childhood and adolescence. Her father, who was an atheist, had abused her mentally and physically. Her mother was a Mormon of sorts, but the dominating influence in their home was anger and depression. By the time she was thirteen, she was a thief and a compulsive runaway; by fifteen she was the leader of a girl's gang in Albuquerque. She experimented extensively with drugs, mostly LSD, but eventually tired of drug experiences. One day she decided to do something different, so she went downtown to the public library, stole one of the books on religion, and took it home to read. This book aroused an interest in the Bible, so she acquired one and began to read it several hours each day. One day she became aware of a living presence that seemed to emanate from its pages, and although she neither saw nor heard anything unusual, she surrendered to that presence. This presence felt as though someone she had known long ago had returned. That is how she describes becoming a Christian.

Deby describes her drug experiences as having magnified or distorted her physical perceptions. If she looked at flowers, they would appear to bloom much more than they normally did; if she watched television, the set would appear to melt. The nature of her drug experiences was such that images in her visual field were always of things she knew to be there, never of nonexistent things. She also experienced flashbacks because of the large amount of LSD she had taken, but these experiences filled her with dread and gave her the sensation of being paralyzed from the neck down. She says the difference between these experiences and the one in which she saw Jesus was like night and day.

Deby was not able to describe in detail the figure she saw in her vision, although she says he seemed average in height and appeared alive and solid. It was not so much his appearance that impressed her, but rather the way he spoke to her and what he said. She was convinced it was Jesus in part because his appearance conformed to traditional images of him, but also because of the transformation that took place before her eyes. She was not aware of any other person in recent times having had a visionary experience. It confirmed her Christian faith and prepared her for the death of her parents that occurred soon afterward and for the challenges of raising a child as a single parent. Deby had completed a first degree in theology when I spoke to her, and was on her way to completing a doctorate in ministry. She has founded a Christian organization for the purpose of helping prison inmates.

Comment

This experience was interesting for several reasons. First, it combined an experience that apparently involved ordinary perception with one that sounds like an out-of-the-body experience. A person skeptical of visionary experiences might think that the experience was really a dream, particularly because it occurred at night while Deby was lying in bed and also because she did lose consciousness. But Deby is adamant about having been awake when the vision began. The second interesting feature is the change in appearance of the figure

Deby saw. I questioned her closely on this matter, and she insisted that the experience definitely did not begin with the radiance that later enveloped the figure. It is also interesting that this transformation contributed to the identification that Deby made.

The third element that is of interest is the unique position Deby was in to compare her drug and flashback experiences with the vision. It is natural to expect that the vision might have been similar to a drug or flashback experience, and perhaps there are cases in which such a comparison might be made, but Deby was quite insistent about the sharp contrast between the visionary experience and the others. Though some might think having taken drugs earlier in life casts doubts on a person's report of a visionary experience, it might be noted that only a person who has experienced both can credibly compare the detailed character, including any differences, between the vision and drug-induced hallucinations.

"Just Focus on Me"

When Maria Martinez was young, she lived with her mother on weekends and with her paternal grandparents during the week. Her family was Roman Catholic, and she attended a Catholic school. Maria's experience occurred as she was walking down the street with her mother. They were waiting to cross a busy intersection when she noticed a tree nearby. It had two trunks, either because two trees had grown together or because the main trunk had divided. As she focused her attention on the tree, she saw that a man—Jesus—was framed by the two trunks. He stood about seven feet away, life-size, and semitransparent, for she could see the traffic through him. Maria does not believe she would have been able to touch him if she had stood near enough. His robe was white, and a red cape rested on his shoulders. His complexion was fair, and he had a beard. He looked at her with gentleness and grace, but also penetratingly.

Maria felt she was being invited to gaze upon him, and as she did so, an extraordinary sense of peace came over her. Because Maria's parents had divorced, she felt a lot of rejection. His message to her was, "You will go through life feeling humiliated, embarrassed, and made a fool of. You will be laughed at, you will be ridiculed, you will not be believed. You are going to go basically through a lot of rejection." Then he added, "If you'll just focus on me, I will see you through this. I will make sure that some day you will be believed, you will be respected, you will be lifted. But you must know that I am with you and you must know that you must focus on me and me alone." He somehow communicated this message to her, although his lips did not appear to move.

He disappeared as quickly as he had appeared, but just before doing so, he raised his hand in a gesture of blessing. His hand was on his heart, with two of his fingers extended, just as he appears in the picture of the Sacred Heart widely circulated among Catholics. Maria explained this move as Jesus giving her a mark by which she could recognize him.

By the time the vision was over, her mother was some distance ahead of her, but it seemed to Maria as though time had stood still. She has carried the sense of love he communicated to her since this experience, which took place in Florida in 1964. Maria lived in Miami when I interviewed her, and worked as a realtor and a volunteer for a Messianic evangelistic organization.

Healed of Epilepsy

Ron Lindsay spent his early years alternating between an orphanage and the home of his grandparents. The neglect and abuse he experienced as a result of being abandoned as a child left him emotionally scarred. After he fell off a swing at sixteen, he began to have epileptic seizures. These seizures compounded his feelings of rejection, insecurity, and fear. It was about this time that he became a Christian. He had attended a Catholic church when he was growing up but did not take his faith very seriously until he became involved with the Youth for Christ organization. He then started attending a Pentecostal church near his home, and this is where his vision took place.

By the time Ron was twenty, his epileptic seizures required him to be hospitalized. For about nine months Ron was in and out of a mental hospital. His medications compounded his feelings of disorientation. He wondered if anyone loved him and consoled himself with the thought that God loved him. As he attended church one Sunday morning in the early fall of 1965, he was startled to see Jesus appear at the front of the church. Ron jumped to his feet and exclaimed, "Jesus, you're here! You're here!" Jesus looked at him with eyes that glistened with compassion, held out his hands in a welcoming gesture, and said, "I love you, and I'm going to heal you." Ron responded with, "Oh! Have you come for me?" Jesus replied, "I've come, and I'm going to heal you."

Jesus stayed there for a few moments, gleaming with radiance, and then disappeared. Ron was specific about some details of the vision, saying Jesus appeared from the waist up, wearing a robe that was off-white in color. He stood some twenty-five to thirty-five feet away, appearing solid and obscuring other objects, with the rest of the room looking normal. His lips moved as he spoke. What made the greatest impression on Ron was the brightness in his eyes, for they spoke of love. The congregation accepted his outburst of surprise without much comment.

The months that followed were difficult. Ron lived in a dark basement room when he was not in the hospital. He would sense what he took to be the presence of God, especially in the mental hospital, but he also sensed evil forces that threatened him with death, particularly in his basement room. The voices would say, "I'm going to kill

you. You're finished. Commit suicide. You know you're done with."
His only solace at these times would come through prayer.

Ron reports that he was healed nine months after his vision.
As he entered his church one night, a voice that he describes as that
of the Holy Spirit said to him, "This is your night." As he went for
prayer at the end of the service, he had another seizure. The voices
said, "I'm going to kill him. He's mine." The people in the church
prayed for him for several hours, and conducted what he describes
as an exorcism. For the first time in a long time he slept well, and
when he got up the next morning he felt different. He felt peace and
joy, and it seemed as though someone with strong arms held him
tight and said to him, "I'll be your father, I'll be your mother, I'll be
everything you have need of. Go in peace." For a minute or so he was
overwhelmed by a presence, and then he yelled, "Oh, Jesus, you're
here again!" For a moment, the outline or shadow of a person's back
was visible, and then it vanished. Ron considers this outline and the
arms that embraced him to have been those of Jesus.

Ron completed his high school diploma after this experience
and took some Bible college courses by correspondence. He eventually became an evangelist, and for many years now has made his
living this way, often sharing his experience with his audiences.

Comment

Ron's experience, like a few others that I have described, seems to
have involved two supernatural forces, not just one. Adding even one
supernatural force into our thought makes explanations much more
complicated; adding two complicates explanations beyond imagination. Historic Christian faith has insisted that two largely invisible
agencies directly and indirectly influence human life and experience,
and some visions, such as Ron's, reveal something of this. The actual
world we live in appears to be much more complex than would be

maintained by those who believe only in natural objects and forces. The principle of simplicity, which asserts that we should postulate the existence of as few things as possible, is very powerful in scientific culture, where it often takes the shape of embracing a theory that has as few vital components as necessary. Following this principle might be commendable, but not at the expense of truth.

"A Little Bit of Eternity"

Margaret Moyse was brought up in a Methodist home in Australia. After completing conventional schooling, she took up the study of art, and by the time she was sixteen, she had left behind the religious beliefs of her parents and was an atheist. One evening, at age 26, as she was having a conversation with her husband and a friend, she felt compelled to turn around and look toward the kitchen behind her. There in the doorway some eight feet away was a figure she immediately recognized as Jesus.

She turned away and then looked back again to discover he was still standing there. He wore a white garment, was of medium height, and had dark hair and a dark complexion. But it was his eyes that particularly caught her attention, for from them flowed a tremendous stream of love. She believes her attention was drawn to his eyes because of her interest as a painter in the human face. The light from the kitchen illuminated him, and he appeared as real as would any person standing there. No radiance accompanied his appearance, nor did he appear to move, and nothing was said. But the absolute stillness of the moment seemed to her like a little bit of eternity. She turned away and looked a third time, but he was gone. Her husband noticed that something had happened, and she told him and her friend what she had seen.

Margaret describes the effect of the experience as having awakened in her the importance of love for others. After this experience, she felt as though the love of Jesus entered her and flowed through her to others. She began to attend an Anglican church, and was active in a church near her home when I interviewed her, for she believed this to be scriptural.

This experience took place in 1952, but it remained as fresh for her as if it had been recent, she said when I interviewed her in 1993. Margaret worked for some years as a nurse, raised a family, and was active in a community-based mental health organization. Her experience took place in Adelaide, Australia, and this is where I interviewed her.

The Man in Sandals

Sheila Dalrymple was brought up on Vancouver Island in British Columbia by a mother who was Presbyterian and a father who was Catholic. Because of these religious differences, Sheila and the other children were brought up without much direct religious influence. Her parents thought they should receive some religious instruction, so they were sent to the United Church.[1] Sheila was interested in religious matters when she married but not involved in religious life at all. When she and her husband moved to Nelson, British Columbia, they attended the United Church, and this is where her experience took place.

As the congregation prayed during a communion service one morning, she saw Jesus walk out of the door of the minister's office. He went to the center of the podium, looked at her, and said, "Live by my commandments." The sandals on his feet made a noise as he walked, just as if he had been an ordinary person walking across the stage. She looked at her friends sitting on either side of her, wondering if they saw what she did, but they did not appear to. She wondered if she was hallucinating, so she looked again to where she had seen Jesus, and he was still standing there. This time he said to her, "I am here," which convinced her the experience was real. She did not hesitate in making the identification.

Sheila was sitting about the fifth row from the front, twenty feet or so away from him, and saw his facial features very clearly. He appeared similar to traditional presentations, but the blue color of the robe he wore was quite unlike anything she had seen before. He was Mediterranean in appearance and had dark hair. He was normal in size and looked solid. The sense of beauty and love that emanated from him was overpowering. Sheila said something extraordinary was present in the atmosphere of the church that she could not explain. It gave her a sense of "weather," but she was not able to be more specific. This "atmospheric effect" made her feel like a grain of sand on the seashore and also suggested he had absolute power. She had a sense of foreboding but was not sure about whether this was communicated via visual effects or whether it was a feeling whose source she could not identify. Sheila also said she had the sense of being confronted by God.

Sheila was haunted by not knowing why this event happened to her. She had not given Jesus much thought prior to this event and did not know why he would concern himself with her. A week prior she had conceived a daughter, who died at birth six months later. Sheila wondered if he was there to strengthen her, for she felt a lot of love and comfort coming from him. Sheila said that Jesus became very real to her through this event and solidified her faith in him.

Comment

Most people who hear about vision experiences want to know what purpose they serve. Those who cannot provide a convincing explanation are sometimes viewed suspiciously, as though the experience could not be genuine if its purpose cannot be given. The visionaries I interviewed often indicated that their experiences brought them to Christian faith, or convinced them Jesus was real, or prepared them for a life of devotion, perhaps even suffering. Another possible purpose of these experiences, however, is simply to witness to the reality of a largely invisible world. This could be the explanation for Sheila's experience, and it is an important one also.

"You Carried the Cross for Me"

Chris was born and raised a Catholic but found religion a source of ambiguity and confusion. The answer people gave to his many questions always seemed to be, "It's a mystery, so don't worry about it." When Chris was twenty-five, he discovered that he had been adopted, and his sense of having been deceived motivated him to move away from home. He was out of work for a while but finally found a job in a convenience store in a small town in Kentucky. All the people in the town seemed to take their religion very seriously, and every street seemed to have a church. A Christian television station had recently begun broadcasting in the area, so Chris began to watch some of its programs. These influences resulted in a search for a meaningful relationship with God.

Working in the convenience store was demanding, for Chris was expected to work ten days in a row before getting two days off. He was sometimes also required to work the night shift. The owner would watch Chris like a hawk as he served the customers, and then accuse him of stealing from the till. On top of everything else, the store was a distance away from the rest of the town, and Chris worried about being robbed. It was patronized mostly by blue-collar workers who worked in factories nearby. They would get their morning coffee and doughnuts at the store before going to work.

Chris was serving a long line of customers at five o'clock one morning when he noticed that a man in line was wearing a shirt and tie. Chris wondered what the man was doing in the store so early in the morning, for he did not seem to be dressed for factory work. Chris did not pay him close attention, as he was preoccupied with pouring coffee and making change. The man was about thirty years old, six feet tall, and had light brown hair and a full beard. He did not fit the stereotype of a community resident, as far as Chris was concerned, because he looked refined, highly intelligent, and very kind and loving. As he stepped up to be served, Chris gave him the customary "Good morning." The man asked for coffee and Chris went behind the counter to pour it.

When Chris returned with the coffee, the appearance of this mysterious customer suddenly changed before Chris's eyes. He turned into someone slightly shorter in stature, with short, black, curly hair, very dark eyes, a perfectly manicured, thin, black beard and very white skin. Chris set the coffee on the counter and was about to ask if he needed a paper bag to carry it out, for many of the customers ordered take-out. But he somehow tripped over his words, and instead of asking the stranger if he wanted a paper bag, said, "You carried the cross for me," with an intonation suggesting surprise. The stranger answered in a soft voice with what sounded like "Sure," picked up his coffee and walked out.

Chris suddenly lost all sense of heaviness, and felt as though he was floating away into an amber light. The euphoria that accompanied the experience was like being drunk. He took hold of himself in order to do his work, but the experience left him changed. All feelings of guilt and inadequacy mysteriously left him. It was only later in the day, when listening to a Christian program in which the speaker talked about Jesus Christ's taking away sin and guilt, that Chris put this interpretation on the event that had transpired. Some years later, after moving to Miami where he met Hasidic Jews, Chris learned that the Hebrew pronunciation of "Jesus" is something like "Yeshua," and began to wonder if the stranger was introducing himself as Yeshua, rather than saying "sure." This event took place in February 1980, when Chris was twenty-seven years old.

The Man in the Fire

Erika was brought up in a small Canadian denomination known as the Apostolic Christian Church, which she described as similar to certain Baptist churches. She was fourteen years old when she experienced what she describes as a vision of Jesus. At the time she was thinking a lot about questions of faith. She wondered, for instance, if she believed in God only because her parents had told her to do so. She thought that she ought to have a greater Christian commitment but could not help wondering if the beliefs she had been taught were somehow dreamed up, rather than founded on fact. She wanted to know for herself that Christ existed.

One evening her youth group at the church had a campfire service. They circled around the large bonfire, and as she looked at it, she saw Jesus walking in the fire. She first saw his profile, and then he turned to look at her with an expression of sorrow, but also compassion. Erika was both shocked and slightly frightened, for she had never heard of such a thing happening in recent times. He was of average height and appeared as he does in traditional portrayals, with shoulder-length hair, robe, and so on. She could not see his feet, because they were obscured by the fire, but he seemed to be solid, for he obscured the fire behind him. After a short while, he disappeared from view. The service ended soon afterward, and a friend who had been sitting on the opposite side came up to her and said, "What just happened to you? I just know that something spiritual just happened to you." Erika did not know how to reply, but it amazed her to think that someone recognized that she had undergone a religious experience. Erika believed she was the only person who experienced the vision, however.

She described this experience as having been a turning point in her life as a Christian. She interpreted the sorrowful expression as reflecting disappointment over her lack of commitment at the time. Although the experience did not result in an immediate and complete commitment to a Christian way of life, she did not doubt the existence of Jesus after that. The experience also proved to be a consolation to her some years later when her parents were killed in an automobile accident. Erika was married and attended Trinity Western University when I interviewed her in 1988.

Comment

Several fascinating features stand out in Erika's experience. The fact that she belonged to a church that did not teach people to expect miracles, in addition to the fact that she was probably too young to have been influenced by competing views on miracles, suggests that she had not been conditioned by her culture to expect a vision. Her experience goes contrary, then, to a common myth about visions, namely, that they occur to those who expect them or are encouraged to expect them. Actually, most of the experiences I researched suggest that these are not brought on by expectations. One can see the merit of not gathering information on visions only from the experiences of those who are deeply religious or are in monastic life or some other form of lifestyle that allows withdrawal from the cares and duties that accompany "ordinary" life.

The second interesting feature of Erika's experience is how it is reminiscent of the experience recorded in the Old Testament book of Daniel, where three faithful Jews were thrown into a furnace for their faith. The Babylonian king, Nebuchadnezzar, reported seeing a fourth man with them, "like a son of the gods" (Dan. 3:25).

The Presence of Jesus

Peter Isaac was retired when I met him, after having taught English, history, and geography in British Columbia high schools for more than thirty years. He reported two experiences in which he was aware of the physical presence of Jesus. The first one took place in a hospital in Kelowna, British Columbia, on March 25, 1964. Peter had been hospitalized twice before because of a bleeding duodenal ulcer, but this time the bleeding was more serious. The doctor who attended him warned he would die without an operation. Peter consented, although it required the removal of three-quarters of his stomach. He reported he had experienced healing in response to prayer on a previous occasion, and as he lay there in his hospital bed, he wondered why his requests for healing had not been heard this time.

Two days after the operation, his wife, Lena, came to visit him; as they were talking quietly to each other, Peter became transfixed by what he saw at the foot of his hospital bed. He said:

> It was a man of average height, but what was different about him was that he was not wearing a shirt nor any other clothing above his waist. On his right side, at waist level, was a large, ugly scar, and he was facing me with a broad smile. It was Jesus. Jesus had come to see me. I knew without doubt that it was him, for he appeared as he did so that I would immediately recognize him.

Jesus appeared to be of average height and build, had no beard, looked solid, but did not move. The experience was just as real to Peter as if a friend had dropped in to see him, apart from the manner of dress. What especially captured Peter's attention was Jesus' smiling, compassionate face, for the smile told Peter that he was loved and understood. Peter says that this image has not faded with time. The look of compassion that Jesus gave him told him he did not need to worry about his recovery. Although his wife, Lena, was with him during this experience, she did not see any of what he reported seeing.

The second time Jesus appeared to him was in an experience on January 10, 1990, that Peter referred to as a vision that began with a dream. He dreamed he was involved, contrary to his will, in a most brutal and cruel murder. Almost killed by the assassins, he began to flee from the scene, begging to be shot because of his reprehensible involvement. Someone came along with a shotgun and shot him in the chest. Even though parts of his body were blown away, he was still alive, crawling along the ground and sobbing in grief. He then woke up, aware of his wife in the bed beside him, but still sobbing uncontrollably.

He tried to bring himself under control so he would not awaken her but could not do so. Suddenly Jesus came toward him, from a distance of about twelve feet away, looking as real as life. Peter described the event as follows: "His form was that of a healthy man dressed in casual clothes, and he had a bit of a brownish complexion. But when he saw me, he was not walking anymore, but was immediately down on the ground beside me and putting his arms around me."

Peter describes this experience as one in which the dream changed into a vision, for when he woke up, the images that had formed the content of his dream remained as real and vivid as they had been in the dream. He knew that he was in his own bed, and that his wife was beside him, but he still had the sense of crawling along the ground in an alley after having been wounded by a shotgun blast. It was in that alley that Jesus came to him, to comfort him, to hold him, and to calm his fears. In his words: "In my mind I was crawling along that alley in the city, knowing at the same time that I was lying in bed. I didn't want to cry so loud that Lena would waken. I can't explain." Peter was unable to say if Jesus looked the same as he had in the first visit.

Peter believes this vision came to him as an answer to the prayer he said before retiring for the night. He had been preparing an adult lesson on the deity of Christ and had asked God to show him why Isaiah refers to Christ as "mighty God." Peter has been a lifelong member of the Mennonite Brethren Church.

The Light

Fran Haskett's experience took place in conjunction with a serious illness that befell her husband, Al, about two years after they married in 1948. An obstruction in his bowel required an operation, and infection in his wounds as well as pneumonia put him on the critical list. Over the next two months, Fran divided her time between the hospital and her job checking policies with a life-insurance company.

Her husband was on her mind day and night, and her waking life consisted of a constant stream of unspoken prayers for his recovery. During this time she began to see her own selfishness—always wanting this or that thing that others around her had—and began to realize that the most important thing a person can have is love for others. A sense of gratitude for what she did have began to develop in her, and it was in this context that her experience took place.

One day after work, Fran was sitting in the bedroom of her home in London, Ontario, thinking about the importance of gratitude and love, when her attention was drawn to a patch of white light six to eight inches in height shining in the corner of the room. There were no windows in the room that could explain why that patch of light six feet away appeared, and she found herself staring at it in disbelief. It began to grow in size, and to her amazement it took the form of a person she immediately identified as Jesus. He appeared as tradition portrays him, but Fran was not able to describe further details of his appearance. He was as real as if an ordinary person had been standing there, and she had no doubt about his identity. Although Fran did not share her experience with many people, she once described it to a Bible teacher whom she greatly respected. He told her that the Holy Spirit, not Jesus, had appeared to her, but she disagreed.

Just as the light had grown to form the image of a grown man, so the image began to dwindle in size until it disappeared, much to Fran's disappointment. But the experience left her convinced that Jesus was alive. She found, moreover, a wave of love coming over her that she could not adequately describe. The hurt and anger she had felt about Al's sickness disappeared, and an understanding about love in life dawned upon her. Fran viewed the experience as one in which God decided to show her that his love for her is complete, and that she should not worry about the events over which she had no control. To her amazement, and that of the doctors who were attending Al, he began to mend so quickly that his recovery seemed miraculous. Fran was seventy-four years old when I interviewed her and has since passed away.

Comment

Fran's experience, like many others that I researched, has an unconventionality about it that perhaps contributes to the suggestion that it happened much as she described. Conventional accounts of visions, if such even exist, would not describe a light growing in size to become a human figure having a normal size. The reports of visions and other extraordinary phenomena that suggest the action of some greater being are always tinged with the suspicion that the person reporting the experience might be fabricating the account. Some people think one test for authenticity is whether an account resembles conventional beliefs about extraordinary events: if the account does, it is likely fabricated; if it does not, it is more likely authentic than not.

I do not know if this is a reliable test for authenticity, for clever people might know about its use and concoct an account that defies convention to make their account acceptable. I consider the issue of authenticity to be best overcome by finding so many independent accounts of similar experiences that rejecting them all seems unreasonable.

"You Can Be Baptized"

Helen Huizinga's experience occurred in connection with her reflections as a Christian about the significance of baptism. She was brought up in the Christian Reformed Church and had been baptized as an infant. She had an opportunity to work with children in a Baptist church near her home, and although the church allowed her to do this work because she was a Christian, church leaders really wanted her to be baptized as an adult. This made her read and think about Christian baptism for a period of about three years. Second baptism was a point of contention between her and some members of her family, however, particularly her husband Joe. She eventually decided that she would like to be baptized, and prayed to God that he would somehow allow this to happen.

Helen went to the Baptist church by herself one Sunday morning, knowing that baptisms would be conducted that day. As the pastor preached, she noticed that the front of the church began to be illuminated with light, and that a cloud was forming. In the midst of the light and the cloud, a human figure appeared. Helen stared at it transfixed, and a voice spoke to her saying, "Helen, you can be baptized now." She immediately identified the person as Jesus and replied (in her mind, not out loud) to him, "Lord, can I really? But what about Joe?" Jesus replied that he would take care of Joe, and then he slowly faded from view. Helen looked around from her seat about five rows from the front to see if anyone gave any indication of having seen what she had seen, but she did not notice anything suggesting that they had.

When the pastor completed his preaching, he went to the vestibule to prepare for the baptismal service. Helen followed him, told him what had just happened, and asked him to baptize her there and then. The pastor complied with her request, and when she told her husband later what she had done, he didn't say a word in objection.

Helen said Jesus appeared to be six to eight feet tall, certainly larger than she expected. He appeared to be solid, not transparent, but Helen could not make out any other details. He seemed to be wearing a long, white robe, for instance, but the features of his face were not sharp, and she could not tell whether he had a beard or whether his hair was long. These details were of secondary significance to her, however, for she was overpowered by what was happening. The glory that emanated from and surrounded him captured her attention. Her response was a combination of joy and awe, for she could hardly believe that Jesus would do such a thing for her. The sense of awe evoked by the experience stayed with her for years, making her feel honored and grateful. Helen was forty years old at the time, and the experience occurred in Richmond, British Columbia.

This was not the first time that Helen sensed the presence of God. When she was thirteen, she lived in the Nazi-occupied Netherlands. Her family sheltered Jews in their home, and she was alone when a house-to-house search was conducted in her town. She saw the soldiers coming down her street and prayed to God for protection. When the soldiers mysteriously passed by her house, she became convinced that God cared for her. Helen was employed as a university library technician before her retirement; in addition, she authored a book and raised a family.

Comment

Readers might have noticed and been surprised by the number of experiences that occurred in my home province of British Columbia. This also surprised me. When I first advertised my interest, I placed my advertisements in a national periodical and did not target BC intentionally. After placing an advertisement in the *New York Times*, which has a large circulation, I was contacted by an advertising company that sells advertisements to other newspapers. For a reasonable fee I had my advertisement placed in more than fifty newspapers in Saskatchewan. However, this venture netted no responses at all. The population of Saskatchewan is about one million, which is about one-quarter of that of BC. However, I am none the wiser about why I found so many people whose experiences occurred in BC, compared to Saskatchewan, since I advertised much less in BC. Did more experiences occur in BC than Saskatchewan? Are the people of Saskatchewan more reluctant than those on Canada's west coast to respond to questions about religious experiences? I do not know the answers.

Jesus is a Real Person

Helen Bezanson's first experience occurred when she was about twenty-one, living in Southern Ontario. She went to the Anglican church as a child, but by the time she married and began a family, she was not interested in religion. Her husband's parents took her to a summer camp meeting sponsored by a Pentecostal church, but she did not really understand what was being preached. It seemed to be coming out of the Bible, so she thought it was acceptable. The service ended with an invitation to pray at the front, and when her mother-in-law suggested that she go, Helen did so to please her. Helen returned on the next three nights, going forward each time for prayer because doing so made her feel better about herself.

As she prayed that fourth night, she felt a warm presence around her and thought that someone had touched her. She opened her eyes to see if anyone was nearby, but no one was close enough to be touching her, so she decided to continue praying. She felt a touch again, this time on one of her hands that was raised in prayer. She opened her eyes again to see if anyone was touching her, and again she saw no one, but then she felt that she ought to look up. Her words to me were: "I looked up, my eyes wide open, and I saw Jesus standing just as clear as I can see you sitting there now, and he had both hands out like this [stretched toward her] and he was smiling as though he was accepting me finally." He made a gathering motion with his hands, as though to show her that he was accepting her, and looked so real and alive Helen thought that others must be looking at him too. She looked around to see if others were paying attention to him, but no one else seemed to notice him. She thought to herself, "What's wrong with them? They're not looking at him." She looked back to see if he was still there, and he was.

He stood there some eight to ten feet away, smiling and moving. He looked much as tradition portrays him, although what caught her attention was his eyes and the motion of his hands. Helen also had the sense that she was looking at God, which gave the visual impression a characteristic that she was not able to describe. Another unusual feature of the experience was that Jesus seemed to be standing on a pedestal or pillar, for he was not standing on the floor and he did not appear to be floating. Moreover, it seemed as though he stood in an oval doorway on the pedestal, and that a radiance or glow emanated from the oval doorway and surrounded him. As she gazed on him, she began talking in another language that she knew nothing about at the time. He gradually faded from view and was gone.

This experience created a desire in Helen to please Jesus as much as she could and to study the Bible. It also convinced her that Jesus was real. Her words were:

He's not just something that you learn about in a Bible, in a Sunday school class. Or it isn't just a story. He showed me that he was real, that he's a real person. He's not just an apparition; he's not a figment of our imagination. Nobody has even been able to tell me since that Jesus isn't real and that he can't make himself known to people, because I saw it myself, and that's all the proof I needed.

Helen's second experience took place thirty years later in the church she was attending on Vancouver Island. A group of people were praying for the healing of a woman in the church, and although everyone else had their eyes closed, Helen thought that she should keep her eyes open. Again she felt a warm presence come over her, and as they prayed, a figure suddenly appeared on the overhead screen at the front of the church.

She blinked her eyes to make sure she was seeing properly, and it was still there. Then she looked around at the others who were praying to see if any of them were looking at the screen, but all of them had their eyes closed. She blinked again and thought to herself, "That's Jesus." He was kneeling on one knee and looking up toward heaven. One of his hands was raised, and blood was running down his back. He again seemed as real as life, even though the image was on the screen. Helen wondered if this was just a picture projected onto the screen, but when she looked to the back of the auditorium, she saw that no one was operating the projector.

As she looked back to the screen, she saw Jesus drop his head and slump. Meanwhile, blood continued to pour down his back. The woman for whom the church was praying was never healed, and Helen thinks there is some connection between this fact and the last scene she saw. Helen said these experiences convinced her of the spiritual realities affirmed by the Christian church.

Comment

I have carefully examined Helen's experience in some detail in a technical article.[2] I focus on her being able to see Jesus each time she faced the front but note that her perception of Jesus did not follow her eyes when she looked back at the audience she knew was there. This feature of her experience cannot be explained as hallucinatory.

Some critics of visions want to say every vision that can be explained as hallucinatory might well have occurred but that reports which cannot be described as a hallucination are not to be trusted. However, this approach is unreasonably skeptical and unfair. If we are to be rational, we cannot accept just those reports we can explain away and reject those that we cannot explain.

Source of Unconditional Love

Maureen Hason had her first visionary experience (her term) when she was twenty-nine years old. She and her husband were living in Kitchener, Ontario, at the time, but they were not happy. They decided to go to a weekend marriage enrichment retreat. The theme on the last day of the retreat was unconditional love, and the advice they were given was to love their spouses unconditionally, as God loves people. This suggestion was not very helpful for Maureen, for she was accustomed to conditional love and did not understand what was meant by unconditional love.

She went back to her room to be alone and to think about the meaning of this kind of love, and as she sat there contemplating this question, Jesus appeared before her open eyes, extending his hands toward her in a gesture of compassion. His face was sad, and although he did not say anything to her, he communicated with his eyes. She could tell by the look on his face that he knew her through and through, and that he loved her.

She saw that she had been living her own life without his help. What his face said was, "I've been here all along. If you would have just come to me I would have been able to help you." At that moment, she understood the Christian doctrine of forgiveness, and the meaning of the Christian belief that Jesus is the Lord of everything. She identified this experience as the turning point in her religious life.

Jesus appeared only from the waist up, but in other respects appeared very much like the traditional images of him; namely, with a white robe, brown hair and beard, pleasing gentle look, and a tanned complexion. But it was the expression on his face that captured her attention, not his physical appearance. This experience took place in March 1982, and by the time I interviewed her in 1988, she had experienced several other visions. I will describe one more.

Maureen and a friend were having lunch in Dutch Mothers, a popular restaurant in Lynden, Washington, when Jesus appeared. They were sitting at a table for four when he suddenly occupied a vacant chair diagonally opposite Maureen. He looked as though he was eager and excited to be there with them, for they had been talking about their faith. He did not say anything audible to her but somehow communicated the thought found in the biblical text, "When two or three are gathered in my name, I am there also." Maureen described this as having her mind opened to understand the Scriptures and compared it to Luke's account of Jesus' opening the minds of his disciples in Luke 24:45. The experience had an air of reality about it for Maureen because Jesus appeared to be solid, and the back of the chair was obscured in just the way it would have been if an ordinary person had been sitting there. Her friend did not see anything, however. Jesus' appearance on this occasion, as on the others, made Maureen weep.

When he disappeared, she became a little giddy as she described to her friend what she had just seen, and somewhat casually said,

"You'd think he'd wear normal clothes if he's coming out to lunch."
Her friend stared at her in disbelief because of her impudence, and
they both "heard" this remark: "That is how you recognize me."
Maureen explained that this simultaneous hearing was not audible.

Maureen has had other experiences of an intense spiritual
nature. She described one that she interprets as an encounter with
God in his throne room. Although it took place one night while she
was asleep, she does not consider it a dream. In the days before it,
she had been reminiscing about the time when she first heard about
God, through a Bible study for children conducted by a woman who
lived on her street. She wanted to repay the woman, and was praying
to God that she might find her and repay her. That night God said to
her, "Your debt is not to Mrs.———, it's to me." He then instructed
her to open up her home to children for a study similar to the one
she had attended as a child.

Maureen said this experience was different from those with
Jesus, for she felt comfortable with Jesus, but from God there was no
escape. Her words were: "There was no reasoning, and he was everywhere. And I remember when he gave me the instruction, I turned
and he was there. And I kept turning, and he was everywhere. It was
like he was air. He just enveloped the whole room. It wasn't a human
figure, and the thought came to me, 'I can't escape God.'" When she
awoke, she felt as though she had been somewhere else.

Maureen has wondered why she has been privileged to have
visions. After the first one occurred, she thought all Christians experienced them and said as much to a friend who had been a Christian for
a long time. She was surprised to discover they are not common. She
has struggled with "spiritual pride" because she has had these experiences while most other people have not and told me she believes she
has them because she is a doubter by instinct and weak in faith.

Degrees of Lifelikeness

I have presented the vision experiences in the last three chapters in such a way that those in Chapter 4 are the least lifelike and those in the next one are most lifelike. However, this continuum is only an approximate one, for every experience has some feature that deviates from ordinary experience in one way or another. I went into this research not knowing exactly what I might expect to find and was surprised to discover that classifying visions proved to be so difficult. The threefold classification that Saint Augustine introduced into Western thought, which continues to be followed by the Catholic Church, does not shed much light on the diverse nature of visions and appearances of Jesus.

One of the most fascinating aspects of these experiences for me is the ways in which they suggest that "another realm" might exist. For people who find religious claims easy to believe, this feature of visions, apparitions, and appearances might not be particularly significant. However, for people who are inclined to think the only world is the ordinary one that is encountered in the normal way through the five senses and doubt a "spiritual world" exists, these suggestions are important. When several of our normal senses, such as sight and touch, operate together in a vision, for example, the implication that is left is that "another world" has been encountered. Even more important than these experiences, however, are those in which the "vision" is simultaneously experienced by various people, for such experiences are so similar to those of ordinary experience, in which the term "real" finds its origin, that it becomes reasonable to claim the object seen in this way is real. I turn, finally, to the experiences that suggest that Jesus as a divine being appeared.

Notes

[1] The United Church of Canada is a union of Methodist, Presbyterian, and Congregationalist churches.

[2] Phillip H. Wiebe, "Critical Reflections on Christic Visions," in *Cognitive Models and Spiritual Maps*, ed. Jensine Andresen and Robert K. C. Forman, special issue, *The Journal of Consciousness Studies, Controversies in Science and the Humanities* 7 (2000): 119–44.

CHAPTER 7

MODERN APPEARANCES

"Take Me with You!"

Barry Dyck was eighteen years old when his vision (his term) of Jesus took place. He was attending a Bible college in British Columbia at the time and had gone to nearby Mt. Baker in Washington state to ski. As he skied that day, his goggles fogged up, and before he knew what was happening he went over a drop-off. When he reached bottom, the back of his skis struck his neck, breaking three vertebrae and herniating one disc. The pain was excruciating as he was taken off the mountain by the ski patrol. He was rushed to Saint Mary's Hospital in Bellingham, where he was placed in a neck brace and traction, and was kept as immobile as possible. During the next week, his ability to see became impaired as the swelling in his head created pressure on his brain. Surgery was planned to relieve the pressure.

In the middle of the night eight days after the accident, Barry woke to find Jesus standing at the end of his bed. Jesus stretched out his arms toward Barry, and Barry immediately sat up. Despite all the equipment that was attached to him and the orders not to move, he grasped the hands of Jesus and begged, "Take me with you." Barry explained that he made this request to die because he was drawn by an indescribable feeling of love. Jesus somehow indicated that satisfying this request was not possible and that everything would be fine. Barry went back to a fitful sleep, and during the night he took off the neck brace that was limiting his movement.

When he woke up the next morning, he was disappointed to discover that he was still alive! But he found that he could see perfectly and that the swelling and pain were gone. He convinced the attending doctor the next day that he was well enough to go home, and the doctor reluctantly agreed. Barry had been expected to be in the hospital for three months and to need a neck brace for an additional eight months. Within three or four days of returning home, he resumed his regimen of running, without any ill effects.

Barry said that X-rays taken by his family doctor in Seattle several weeks later showed no evidence of fracture in his neck vertebrae, and that the many X-rays taken during the week in the hospital had shown obvious signs of fracture. Barry believes he was healed by Jesus during the encounter, which lasted no more than sixty seconds. Barry's family and the people in the church they attended were as shocked by Barry's healing as he was. Although the church he attended did not deny the possibility of miraculous interventions, it did not encourage people to expect them.

Barry says Jesus seemed to be about six feet in height and that his hair extended six inches below his shoulders. Barry says the overall impression of his face was like Warner Sallman's *Head of Christ*,[1] but he could not see any features in detail. Barry could see the hair draped around the face, but it was as if the face of Jesus were hollow. Barry does not know how he identified the radiant figure as Jesus, but it came to him immediately and without any question or doubt. The experience convinced him he was loved, but he thinks the incident may have had another purpose. He has often shared his experience with other people and influenced them to think about God and spiritual life generally. Barry went to a college to study science for three years after completing that year in Bible college, and he pursued further studies in accounting after that.

Comment

In Barry's healing, we are introduced to an event that happened in the ordinary world of space and time. This means that something occurred for which an explanation is required, which goes beyond the images that people see in visions. Moreover, because Barry's vision occurred along with his healing, and preceded it, we can plausibly view the vision and the healing as linked together in some way—if not as cause and effect, then as effects of a single cause.

Up to this point in the visions that I researched, I have described experiences that belonged largely to the private world of visionaries, but with Barry's experience the invisible spiritual world seems to have penetrated our ordinary world—the space-time-causal world—and left a trace in it that can be examined. I spoke to friends of Barry from that time who verified his claim that he had been involved in a skiing accident and had recovered incredibly quickly.

I personally do not think that we can be presumptuous in describing the exact character of that normally invisible world that is encountered in these experiences. However, the external observer, not just the person with the vision, is entitled to say that something real has been encountered, even if it cannot be fully described.

Combined Touch and Sight

John Occhipinti was brought up in a very devout home in Connecticut and New Jersey. His mother went to the Catholic church every day to pray and also attended the services of the Assemblies of God. John was a special child because of an incident that took place when he was two years of age. He fell into the river just behind their home and was not rescued for more than half an hour. John was rushed to hospital, where doctors worked for hours to save his life, so his mother was convinced that there was a special reason for his survival. John became serious about his faith when he was about eighteen years old. The next year he went to Bible college in Texas to prepare for pastoral work, and in 1958, his experience took place there.

John shared a room with Nathan but could not understand what Nathan was doing in Bible college, for he already seemed to know most of what they had come there to learn. During November of that year, Nathan came down with a virus and stayed in bed to recover. Nathan was not particularly perturbed about being sick, but said that he was in bed for a reason. Although this was not a serious illness, John felt sympathy for him and brought him food from the cafeteria when he could and prayed with him before retiring for the night.

As he was praying for Nathan one night, he opened his eyes to look at his friend lying about eight feet away. John was shocked to see someone standing over Nathan's bed, but facing and looking at him. John immediately identified the person as Jesus, in part because of the sense of awe that his appearance evoked. John was about to tell his sick friend what he was seeing when Jesus reached over and placed his hand on Nathan's forehead and disappeared. At that instant, Nathan leaped out of bed and ran down the halls of the dormitory shouting, "I've been healed, I've been healed."

Nathan later said that he did not see anyone, but he felt something touch his head. John himself intended to go over to touch Jesus in order to establish his reality for himself but did not get a chance to do so. He later mused about his boldness, but he was only nineteen at the time, and rather new in his faith.

Jesus appeared much as tradition portrays him, with a long white robe, shoulder-length hair, and a short beard. He seemed to be just under six feet tall. He exhibited no radiance, and he seemed as solid as any ordinary person. His skin was neither very dark nor very light, but his eyes seemed to be on fire. John preferred the term *encounter* rather than *vision* to describe the experience. It was as real to him as seeing an ordinary person, and he did not think that Nathan would have felt the touch on his head if it had been a vision. Moreover, John did not consider experiences seen with open eyes to be visions. He was not aware at the time of anyone else in recent times having had such an experience. John considered the experience to have had two purposes: to bring healing to his friend and to reaffirm John's desire to do evangelistic work. John was active as an evangelist, a counselor, and a musician when I met him in 1991.

Comment

Combined sight and touch are very important in establishing that something whose existence might be considered dubious is real. Many people have been to science museums and seen what lasers can do in creating holograms—three-dimensional images that seem to float in space. Most people want to reach out to touch the image, but of course they are unable to feel anything. If we were to try to squeeze the "object" that we seem to see, we would find our thumb and forefinger touching. The "object" that is seen is not where it is seen, but in some other place. Our visual sense almost fools us momentarily, unless we are familiar with holograms, into thinking that something exists that does not. When sight and touch combine to give us the combined visual impression and the feel of an object, we think that the seen and felt object must be real. We could say that the sense of touch (the tactile sense) is sometimes as important as the visual sense in establishing what is real.

The experience of John is extraordinary for he wanted to verify what he saw was real by touching it, which is an instinctive reality check. However, he was not allowed to do so, but his friend, to whom I did not speak since John had lost contact with him, was the one who evidently felt what John saw.

Lakeshore Gospel Chapel

Kenneth Logie's life was marked by a number of extraordinary experiences. He was the minister of a Pentecostal Holiness church in Oakland, California, for many years,[2] and the reports of events that emanated from it rival the New Testament in kind and number.[3] Among these are various encounters with Christ, including several claims of group experiences.

When Kenneth and his wife moved to Oakland, the church was not capable of fully supporting them financially, so he sold bread to supplement his income. His work sometimes meant he was late for the evening service, but the small congregation accepted that, and he would simply begin his preaching a little later than usual when this happened. One Sunday night in April 1954, he again arrived late and, as a result, was still preaching at 9:15 when he saw a shadow on the exterior glass doors, made by someone standing outside. He wondered who might be arriving so late in the evening. He reported that "the door opened up, and Jesus started walking down the aisle just as plain as you are." He turned to the people on one side of the aisle, and then to the people on the other side of the aisle, smiling as he went. He walked up to the platform where Kenneth was preaching, but instead of walking around the pulpit, moved right through it. When he placed his left hand on Kenneth's shoulder, Kenneth collapsed to the floor. Jesus then knelt down alongside him and spoke to him in another language. Kenneth responded in English, believing he was interpreting what was being said to him. He says this event was witnessed by the congregation of about fifty people present on that occasion.

Kenneth reported another incident that took place in May 1959 in the same church. People who came to the services were encouraged to report important events in their lives, and one day a woman in the congregation described a vision she had seen when she was in a hospital and was thought to have died. Mrs. Lucero reported that Jesus appeared to her in this vision wearing the clerical robe of a Catholic priest and told her to have faith in God. She explained that because she was of Catholic background, this apparel somehow assisted her in making the identification of the figure as Jesus.

Kenneth said when Mrs. Lucero got up to tell her story, she was wearing a black raincoat because the weather had been rainy that day. As she spoke about the vision she had experienced about a week earlier, she disappeared from view, and in her place stood a figure taken to be Jesus. He wore sandals, a glistening white robe, and had nail prints in his hands—hands that dripped with oil. Kenneth reports that this figure was seen by virtually everyone in the congregation, which he estimated at 200 people. He also reports that the figure was filmed (in color) by the church organist with the kind of eight-millimeter movie camera popular at the time. Kenneth says the organist was so awestruck that he shook and placed the camera on top of the organ in order to keep it steady. The appearance of the man was much like Sallman's *Head of Christ*. Kenneth says the effect upon the people in the church was electrifying. After several minutes, Jesus disappeared and Mrs. Lucero was again visible.

Comment

These allegations put encounters with Jesus into the space-time-causal domain and, if authentic, would challenge the dominance of naturalism within the scientific community. They would also challenge the religious beliefs of many people, including Christians. I shall elaborate on the second case in some detail because of its significance.

The circumstances surrounding the film were described to me in 1965 by Kenneth Logie and his wife, both in a public meeting in Grenfell, Saskatchewan, when I saw the film, and in private conversation. I was a young undergraduate at the time and was not comfortable with the thought of giving the film or the supposed incident any attention. I did not speak in detail with Kenneth about these events again until 1991, by which time his first wife had died. I visited him and the church that summer and spoke with four or five people who had been present in his church in 1959 when the incident took place. They supported the account given above.

I naturally wanted to see the film again, primarily to refresh my memory concerning what I had seen twenty-six years earlier, and was disappointed to learn that it had been stolen from the apartment in which Kenneth lives. I estimate that there were about two hundred people present in the public meeting in Grenfell when I saw the film. I do not know how often it was shown in public, but my impression is that Kenneth showed it in his church from time to time. The woman involved in the incident, Mrs. Lucero, who was already quite old at the time it took place, died a few years later.

My own memory of the film is that it showed a figure that looked like traditional images of Jesus. The woman in the black raincoat did not appear, to my recollection. My memory of the glistening white robe as well as the outstretched and scarred hands is clear, but I cannot remember any movement of the figure, nor do I remember seeing the full face appear. Kenneth, who naturally saw the film a number of times, says the face appeared on the film. Joy Kinsey, whose experience was recounted in an earlier chapter, was a member of the church at the time and says his memory of the content of the film is correct. I cannot account for my slightly different memory of what I saw, but I was quite terrified by the allegations that were made, so that might have affected my recall. It is well-known that people who have been present to witness a single event can have different memories of what occurred.

People offer competing views, naturally, on how the film was produced or what it represents. Some people of course believe that it recorded a supernatural event. Others say the whole thing was fraudulent, that an actor was hired to play the part, and that an amateur photographer filmed it. But I am sure they reached this conclusion without investigating the circumstances surrounding it. One person who regularly attended the church about the time of the alleged event, but was not present at the event and saw the film only later, told me he wondered whether the film might have been of a painted portrait of Jesus. My own recollection is that there was movement on the film of various members of the congregation that could not be explained by motion of the camera. The suggestion that it was produced by trick photography seems dubious to me, because its production in 1959 probably predates the easy availability of the required equipment, and it had the amateurish quality that home movies from that era generally have.

There is quite a bit more to the Oakland context than so far suggested. It is natural to wonder, for example, why someone would have had a movie camera in the services. Kenneth says the church went through a period of extraordinary healings, exorcisms, prophesies, and so on—he has dozens of fascinating accounts. He reports an experience, for instance, in which the roof of the church was bathed in visible but non-consuming fire, causing the neighbors to call the fire department. He also reports that images of crosses, hearts, and hands mysteriously appeared on the walls of the church, and from these flowed streams of liquid having the consistency of oil. The appearance of these images coincided with fragrant aromas that seemed to come from them. This was the context in which the Oakland apparition experiences described above supposedly took place. Kenneth said he did not know what to expect next in the life of his church and so bought the home movie camera in the hope that he might record any noteworthy incident.

The accounts Kenneth gave of various wonders and miracles that were part of his church for a number of years are reminiscent of New Testament accounts, for of course the Gospels and Acts are full of accounts of such phenomena. In 1991 Kenneth showed me black and white photographs of the images that had appeared on the walls. He also had photographs of one or two occasions during which stigmata appeared on his hands and another of a white cross that once appeared on his forehead. I asked him about the stigmata, and he said that these had occurred perhaps nine or ten times during a period of about three years, and were accompanied by a burning sensation, as if his hands were on fire. He was understandably sympathetic to similar claims that have been made over the centuries, by Christians of all persuasions, and he showed me a few newspaper clippings and photographs he had collected that featured similar incidents from various Christian traditions.

I am not aware that any attempt has been made to document the events alleged to have taken place in this small church in Oakland, although people in the church told me in 1991 that they had been visited quite often by reporters and cultural anthropologists. The time gap between the alleged events in Oakland and the time that I visited the Church—about thirty-five years—corresponds quite well to the number of years widely believed to separate the alleged incidents central to the Christian faith and the first gospel narratives of them. Consequently, dismissing the authenticity of the 1950s events in Oakland simply because too much time passed before they were reported would cast a similar negative perspective against the New

Testament's authenticity. The nature of evidence is such that a particular judgment about what is reasonable or unreasonable can be generalized to a different case that is similar to the first.

A group apparition experience is remarkable in itself, but the photographic images are perhaps more remarkable, for a witness's internal mental or neurophysiological mechanisms cannot be plausibly suggested as an explanation for the photos. The suggestion that telepathic powers might somehow account for such images is as challenging to a naturalistic understanding of the world as any supernaturalistic explanation, so any suggestion that telepathy might have been involved will not work in order to avoid abandoning a naturalistic outlook. It is curious to note how some psychical researchers insist that apparitions are not photographable.[4] This position does not tally with an article titled "Ghosts" in *Man, Myth and Magic: An Illustrated Encyclopedia of the Supernatural*, in which author Richard Cavendish asserts that hundreds of still photographs portray what are said to be ghosts.[5] Half a dozen or so are reproduced in the article, and they include some indefinite shapes that are in keeping with various popular ideas of how ghosts might appear. The article also includes several semitransparent human shapes and a photograph of cherubs with wings hovering over a child's bed.

There evidently is no agreement among people who investigate paranormal phenomena about whether such events can be photographed. Perhaps nothing can be established beyond reasonable doubt concerning the Oakland experience, in view of the unavailability of the film for critical scrutiny, but the number of claims emanating from this single locale make it worthy of serious study.

Additional Cases

I will briefly comment on several other visions of Jesus. Two accounts came from people with whom I could conduct only brief and incomplete interviews, and two came from people with whom I was unable to make direct contact, but who are well-known to acquaintances of mine. I present these four cases separately from the accounts of the people with whom I was able to establish direct and significant contact. The two with whom I conducted brief interviews are well-known public figures and authors.

Hugh Montefiore, now deceased, was an instructor in New Testament at Cambridge University and later a bishop of the Church of England. He was brought up in the Jewish faith as a child and never attended Christian worship or read the New Testament. He credits his conversion to Christianity to a vision he experienced at sixteen years of age. The figure that appeared to him said, "Follow me." Hugh told me that he knew the figure was Jesus and thus decided to embrace the Christian faith, although he says he has not ceased to be a Jew. Only later did he discover that the invitation "Follow me" was in the New Testament. When I spoke to him in 1993, some fifty-seven years had elapsed since the incident, so he was not able to remember many of the details of the experience. However, he said the import of the experience still had validity for him. "For me it has total reality," he said.

John White, also deceased, was associate professor of psychiatry at the University of Manitoba for many years and was well-known in Canadian Christian circles for the books he wrote. He said he once saw the arms and hands of Christ extended toward him as he was in prayer with some of his friends. His comments on this experience were significant: "The effect was overwhelming. All strength left me, so that it was with difficulty that I remained kneeling. I began to sweat profusely and to tremble uncontrollably."[6] He went on to say that he was "fully aware that what I saw was a product of my own brain. I felt that God was, as it were, using my mind as a projectionist uses a projector. The hands I saw were not the real hands of Christ: They were weak and effeminate, whereas I knew that the hands should have shown the evidence of manual toil. They weren't carpenter's hands." He went on to remark that the wounds of the crucifixion were in the palms, not the wrists, where they should have been if they had been the hands of Christ, for Romans nailed those they crucified in the wrists, not the hands.

John spoke to me of another experience that had taken place in Honolulu several weeks before I interviewed him in October 1990. He was sitting on a settee, and was wondering what it would be like to have Jesus sit with him. He said Jesus was suddenly there, sitting at the other end of the settee, although he could see Jesus only in outline and could see through him. Jesus sat there for a moment, and then raised his arm and placed his hand on John's left hand that rested on the back of the settee. After a while, Jesus stood up to go, and John said, "Please don't go; stay." But this request was not granted. While Jesus sat there on the settee, John was unable to see his eyes, but when Jesus got up to leave John saw them. He interpreted this as indicative of some unconscious reluctance to get too close to Jesus, and he described this experience as one in which he felt that he was "penetrating into the beyond."

John White's remarks to me about hallucinations were fascinating, for his experience with patients in psychiatric hospitals has given him a rare perspective on the experiences of those who hallucinate. He said his impression was that the hallucinations of those in psychiatric hospitals could possibly be their encounters with evil forces, but he did not think that such a hallucinatory experience implied a person was demonically controlled. He thought that psychoses left the psychotic vulnerable to the "dark world," and that such people might be encountering other realities in visual terms.

His position on this point is similar to one expressed by Sergius Bulgakov, who was a professor of theology at an Orthodox seminary and a popular teacher of the theology of the Orthodox Church in the early part of the twentieth century. Bulgakov writes: "It cannot be affirmed that all mental maladies are of a spiritual nature or origin, but neither can it be affirmed that demoniac influences have no connection with mental maladies; what is called hallucination may be considered—at least sometimes—as a vision of the spiritual world, not in its luminous, but in its dark aspect."[7]

John White's impression was that those who had unusual experiences in two sensory domains at once, for example, visual and tactile, were not simply hallucinating, but he acknowledged that other psychiatrists would look at this phenomenon differently. He said he regards the hallucination theory as just as theoretical as the idea that there is a spiritual world into which some people can see. It is apparent that he is using the concepts coming from various competing explanations, each with its own characteristic view of what is real.

The final two visions of Jesus in this chapter came to my attention through acquaintances, people who know the principal persons well. Both experiences involve healings, and have already been published. Betty Jean Baxter has very widely recounted her experience of having been healed by Jesus when she was twelve from a condition of being crippled and deformed. Her mother and several other people were present at this event, and reportedly also saw Jesus perform the healing. Betty describes details of trying to touch Jesus as he stood before her, of a friend reprimanding him for standing too far away, of seeing a vision of Jesus "repairing" a deformed tree within this experience, and finally of being healed as he placed his hand upon her severely deformed spine. Her story was reported in *The Fairmont Daily Sentinel* in Fairmont, Minnesota in 1952, according to the dust jacket of a recording.[8] Her story is now available on *The Pathfinder* website, which includes an audio file of Betty describing her healing.[9]

Gulshan Esther reports having been healed after an apparition of Jesus at a time of her life when she was a devout Muslim and her only knowledge of Christianity was the little information found in the Quran.[10] She had been crippled by typhoid when only six months old. Gulshan claims Jesus and his apostles all appeared to her nineteen years later, and that she was taught the Lord's Prayer during this encounter. It was her knowledge of this prayer that convinced a Christian missionary in Pakistan to risk his right to stay in the country to teach her. Gulshan now lives in Oxford, England, and conducts frequent missions to Pakistan. This case is unusual inasmuch as Gulshan's knowledge of Christian beliefs seems to have been very limited before the encounter, and it presents interesting evidence about how previous knowledge shapes the actual content of a visionary's experience.

In concluding this study of visions of Jesus, I will turn to the problem of determining how he appeared in real life.

Notes

[1] See the next chapter for a discussion of this famous painting.

[2] This is the same church where Joy Kinsey reported the experience described in Chapter 4.

[3] See Kenneth Logie, *Stepping Stones to Glory* (New York: Vantage Press, 2001) for many accounts.

[4] For example, G. N. M. Tyrrell, *Apparitions* (London: Gerald Duckworth, 1942), 8f.

[5] Richard Cavendish, "Ghosts" in *Man, Myth and Magic: An Illustrated Encyclopedia of the Supernatural*, ed. Richard Cavendish (New York: Marshall Cavendish Corp., 1970).

[6] John White, *Putting the Soul Back in Psychology* (Downers Grove, Ill.: Intervarsity, 1987), 87.

[7] Sergius Bulgakov, *The Orthodox Church* (Crestwood, NY: St. Vladimir's Seminary, 1988), 128.

[8] Betty Baxter, *The Betty Baxter Story: A 1941 Miracle as Told by Herself*, ed. Reverend Don Heidt (Garden City, NY: Country Life Press, 1951), from the Foreword by Oral Roberts, 1.

[9] "The Betty Baxter's [sic] Story," *The Pathfinder*, accessed December 18, 2013, http://godfire.net/betty_baxter.htm.

[10] Esther, *Torn Veil.*

CHAPTER 8

THE SHROUD OF TURIN AND OTHER IMAGES

One of the remarkable aspects of early Christian documents is that none of them provide an account of how Jesus looked in real life. Despite that lack of description, a strong tradition of how he appeared has arisen in Western culture, so anyone who uses an image to illustrate children's stories or hires an actor to depict him for a movie can readily reinforce that image. Of course, they could also challenge it, but they seldom do. Jesus is often portrayed as being of about average height, with long hair and a full beard, wearing a long robe, and perhaps with brown eyes and a sallow complexion in order to give him a "Mediterranean look." Whether this image is correct is difficult to answer, but it is certainly a controversial topic.

The question of how Jesus appeared in real life seems to be in the minds of those who challenge visionaries to provide a description of what they actually saw, including the face and other physical features.

If the description a visionary provides is very different than the traditional image, the experience is likely to be written off as illusory; if the description conforms to the traditional image, it might be written off as merely the result of previously formed beliefs. At some point in the discussion of "authentic" visions of Jesus, questions inevitably arise about how well or how poorly a visionary's description matches the traditional likeness of Jesus.

I mentioned in Chapter 1 that the form in which Jesus appeared after his resurrection might have varied. If his form did vary, and perhaps continues to do so if he indeed continues to appear to people, then establishing how Jesus appeared before his death might have little relevance to questions about the "authenticity" of a vision. Even if his appearance in visions is not central to questions of authenticity, however, the question of how Jesus looked in real life still is interesting. In this chapter, I will explore some unique images that purport to reveal how Jesus looked, and some unusual experiences that have been reported in conjunction with attempts to paint his likeness.

The Shroud of Turin

Perhaps the most significant recent claim about how Jesus looked comes from research into the Shroud of Turin. Some claim that this is the cloth used to wrap the body of Jesus after his death and that it somehow captured an image of how he appeared at that time. I cannot give this important topic the attention it deserves in this kind of study, for more than two dozen academic disciplines are now involved in the study of the Shroud, making answers to questions about its properties and origins extraordinarily complex. Fortunately, many books have been written recently on the topic, and well-researched documentaries have appeared on television, so further information on the Shroud is easy to obtain. Consequently, my remarks here will be brief.

Several facts about the Shroud have received much publicity, including the fact that the image of the man as it appears on the Shroud has reversed light and dark, much as a film negative does (see Plates 8.1 and 8.2). Another well-known piece of information is that the carbon-dating tests conducted on it 1988 suggested that the Shroud originated in the thirteenth or fourteenth centuries of our era, not in the first.

Many suggestions about how the image was produced on the Shroud have been put forward, among them the idea that an artist might have produced it. However, good reasons exist to doubt that it is the work of an artist, which are discussed in the following list.

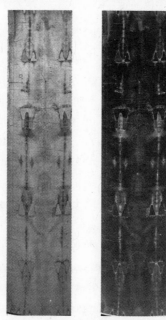

PLATE 8.1. On the left is the Shroud as it appears in real life; on the right is the photographic negative of it.

PLATE 8.2. The face of the man on the Shroud
in positive (left) and negative (right).

- Hungarian artist Isabel Piczek, who has painted the human form, often on large murals, for more than forty years, says the anatomical perfection exhibited on the Shroud could not be painted today, even with the aid of a camera. The minuscule color variations that form the image are all done without any visible outlines on the cloth, and in such a way that light and dark are reversed.[1]
- The color variations on the fibers that form the image are so delicate that if the image were painted, an artist would have to have used a brush with only one hair in it, and that thinner than a human hair.[2] The optimal viewing distance is six to ten feet away, and at less than six feet the image almost disappears.[3] An artist would have to have stood a considerable distance away to produce even a slightly plausible figure—all in the form of a photographic negative.

- The fibers of the cloth are not cemented, which they would have been if paint had been used to produce the image.[4]
- No substantial paint, dye, or stain residues have been found on the Shroud.[5]
- Microscopic examination of the face image reveals no preferred direction, but a painter could not have avoided showing some preference in brush strokes.
- The Shroud's image has a three-dimensional character, when viewed with an instrument that was originally designed by NASA to interpret certain kinds of black-and-white images of the Earth taken from space. This three-dimensional feature of the image cannot be replicated even with today's technology.
- A medieval artist would likely have painted the hands with thumbs, rather than without them. The absence of thumbs is now known to be consistent with damage to the radial nerves in the wrists, which results in the thumbs flexing into the palms.
- High levels of bilirubin occur in the blood found on the Shroud. Bilirubin is a chemical that turns the bile pigments reddish-orange in color, and is indicative of severe jaundice, often brought on by physical trauma. It is unlikely that a medieval forger thought of adding bilirubin to the image in order to give it a lifelike quality, since its existence has only come to be known in the last century.
- The dorsal (back) foot imprint has an abundance of microscopic dust, atypical of the rest of the image. An artist would not likely have added this element, for he or she could not have seen the dust, and would have had no

reason to put the dust there since no one else could see
it either.[6]

The large amount of blood found on the Shroud suggests that a
man once lay between the two halves of this fourteen-foot length of
cloth, and that much of the blood got onto the cloth by contact with
a body. Doubts about the presence of blood were once expressed,
but these seem to have disappeared. Research during the early part
of the twentieth century concentrated on the apparent congruity
of the apparent wounds of the man on the Shroud with those said
in the gospels to have been inflicted on Jesus. Although the image
appears somewhat obscure to the naked eye, photographs of the
whole Shroud have allowed forensic pathologists to observe the
blood stains on the cloth in relation to various features of the image
itself. The following features have been observed.

- The Shroud exhibits blood flows from hands and feet, as
  from nailing. These correspond to the wounds of crucifixion described in the Gospels.
- Pathologists also say the Shroud indicates that the victim
  was flogged, and close measurements of the wounds
  reveal that the instrument apparently used is consistent
  with relics preserved from the Roman era used to carry
  out this form of torture. The Gospel accounts say Jesus
  was subjected to this cruelty prior to his crucifixion.
- The Shroud shows that the victim has injuries to his head,
  as from a crown (or cap) of thorns. The gospels explain
  that this was devised for Jesus, probably uniquely, perhaps to ridicule the claim that he was a king, and has
  been widely considered a strong reason for thinking the
  man on the Shroud might be Jesus.

- The Shroud shows the victim did not have his legs broken, contrary to the usual practice in crucifixion. Some researchers think victims of crucifixion died of asphyxiation, as the weight of their own bodies hanging by their hands made breathing difficult, and exhaustion finally prevented them from raising their chests sufficiently to take a breath by pushing down on their impaled feet. In a final act of mercy, executioners would break the victim's legs so asphyxiation would come quickly. John's gospel says Jesus' legs were not broken, offering one more point of congruity with the Shroud.

- The victim depicted on the Shroud has the blood of a human male, for both X and Y chromosomes have been found. The blood is of the AB type, which is found in only 3.2 percent of the world's population, but is found in 18 percent of the Jewish people in the Near East.[7]

- The victim depicted on the Shroud appears to have had a chin-band tied around his head, which is consistent with some Jewish burial practices.[8] John makes reference to a cloth that was around the head of Jesus.

- The victim depicted on the Shroud seems to have had his heart pierced by a sharp object, for images appear on the back that correspond to blood and "water" (serous fluid).[9] The Gospel of Saint John says Jesus had his heart pierced.

- Pathologists say the person on the Shroud was between thirty and thirty-five years old, which is consistent with information available from the New Testament about the age at which Jesus was crucified.

These items, like many others that researchers have advanced, vary in force as far as establishing the identity of the man on the Shroud.

For example, the fact that the image depicts one who was crucified does not uniquely identify Jesus as the man on the Shroud, since many people were crucified in antiquity. However, the fact that the image depicts one who had an apparently unique implement of torture placed on his head, such as a crown of thorns, goes a long way to make the identification of the person as Jesus. Moreover, the evidence provided by any one of these items might not be that significant, but the combined effect of them in reinforcing the accounts in the Gospels is impressive.

Several other points about the Shroud should be noted, although their value as evidence for the identity of the man in the image is modest.

- Coins appear to have been placed over the eyes of the victim depicted on the Shroud, in keeping with common burial practice in Judea during the first half of the first century. The first coin was reported in 1979 by a theologian at Loyola University in Chicago and confirmed in 1985 by an Italian coin expert.[10] The existence of a second coin was reported in 1996 by a medical examiner from the University of Turin, along with an expert in computer enhancement from the same institution. Enlargements of the inscriptions appear to indicate that these coins were minted during the reign of Tiberius Caesar—29 A.D. in our system of dating.[11] This item of evidence is remarkable, for it is difficult to imagine how an image on a rather porous piece of cloth, rather than photographic film, could yield such detail, and some commentators treat the claim with caution, preferring to regard the alleged coin images as only a quirk of the Shroud's weave.[12]

- Forty of the pollen grains found on the Shroud are from plants growing exclusively in Israel. This implies that the Shroud was exposed to the open air in that country, since this is the usual way in which pollen becomes embedded in the fibers of a piece of cloth. While an extreme skeptic could argue that pollen from Israel might have been borne to Europe by the wind, this claim goes beyond the bounds of plausibility, for the prevailing winds in Europe are not from east to west. This fact points to Israel as the place of origin of the Shroud.

- A faint outline of a flower garland has been detected among the various images on the Shroud. Paul Maloney says he found a chrysanthemum-shaped flower, and an Israeli botanist has confirmed the presence of plants in this garland exclusive to Israel, providing still more evidence that the Shroud has been in Israel.[13] This finding is even more significant than the pollen grains, for the process by which the body image was formed seems to have been the same that resulted in the image of the flower garland, suggesting that they were produced at the same time. This would place the origin of the Shroud in Israel.

- The dust found in the area of the feet contains limestone of the relatively rare aragonite variety, rather than the common calcite variety. The limestone has small quantities of iron and strontium, but no lead, and corresponds to limestone found in tombs near Jerusalem.[14]

The various items of evidence advanced to this point are not conclusive about the identity of the person depicted on the Shroud, but they do point in the direction of Jesus. The Shroud unquestionably has its origins somewhere in Europe or the Middle East, most likely the

Middle East. Moreover, Jesus is one of the few people whose method of execution and appearance in death has been celebrated by his followers. The claim that the victim is Jesus has plausibility. Of course, the carbon dating test performed on the Shroud in 1988 seems to put its origin in about the thirteenth century, and so undermines the claim that the image is that of Jesus.

Researchers have puzzled about this carbon-dating result, for it is obviously inconsistent with the evidence suggesting the man is Jesus. Other features of the image are also difficult to explain, such as the three-dimensional character of the image. Another is that the image is formed by extremely small pixel-like dots, resembling pointillism in art, although in the case of the Shroud the dots are microscopic in size. These dots have been formed by what appear as chemical burns to the tiny fibrils that form the threads of the cloth. This feature suggests that the image was produced by bombardment of some sort. Other peculiarities include the surface character of the image so that the image is seen only on one side of the cloth,[15] the absence of side images of the man, and the vertical alignment of the image and associated body parts such as the face, legs, and hands.

Still another anomaly is the odd locations of some of the blood residues on the Shroud, which seem to have gotten onto the cloth by contact with the man. Some of the blood residues, for example, appear to be on the hair on the head of the man, but this does not seem the right location for them, since the location is too far away from a possible point of bleeding. Another peculiarity associated with the blood spatters on the Shroud is that the blood-impregnated fibers exhibit no evidence of fraying. Other puzzling features of the Shroud image are the man's elongated fingers and a spot on one of the hands that seems to register the presence of a thumb folded into the palm. More controversial are the claims that faint images of teeth, vertebrae, metacarpal bones in the wrists, and other bones can be seen.[16] The question that researchers are confronted with is what conjecture might explain all or most of these puzzling features of the Shroud.

Physicist John Jackson, long associated with research into the Shroud, has conjectured that the body of the man in the Shroud "became mechanically 'transparent' to its physical surroundings," and that "a stimulus was generated that recorded the passage of the cloth through the body region onto the cloth as an image."[17] Recently deceased historian of physics, Thaddeus Trenn, describes the essential element in Jackson's obscure explanation as "weak dematerialization." Trenn suggests that the nuclei of the atoms constituting the body of the man once wrapped in the Shroud broke apart.[18] The freed subatomic particles formed a flux through which the Shroud fell, by virtue of the gravitational force acting on the cloth.[19] These particles left their "imprint" on the cloth, so the color variations that form the image resulted from the number of subatomic particles that bombarded the cloth—the fewer the number of particles, the lighter the image (on the original cloth), and the larger the number of particles, the darker the image. This conjecture would explain the pointillism, the three-dimensional effect, the absence of torn fibrils in the area of the blood stains, the alignment of parts of the body with elements of the image, the absence of side images, and the faint images (possibly) of bones and the thumb inside the palm.

Trenn argues that this theory postulates a "radiation event" that could account for the medieval carbon dating claimed in the 1988 test, for the theory implies that freed neutrons from the nuclei would have converted some of the nitrogen in the linen that forms the Shroud into carbon-14, thereby producing sufficient additional amounts of this isotope to make the Shroud look medieval rather than ancient. Trenn observes that this theory is testable, for an implication is that the carbon-14 amounts would vary over the surface of the cloth. Cloth in the immediate vicinity of the image would have a higher concentration of carbon-14 than cloth on the edges. This implication has not been tested, to my knowledge, although one statistician has reported that a statistically significant variation is already evident in the results from the three laboratories that carbon-dated the Shroud in 1988.[20] The Oxford laboratory reported a smaller amount of the carbon-14 isotope, on which carbon-dating results depend, than the laboratories in Tucson and in Zurich. The sample sent to Oxford was just slighter farther from the image of the man than the samples sent to the other laboratories, so this result is consistent with Jackson's theory.

This brief discussion of the Shroud indicates something of the difficulties involved in interpreting the evidence capable of being gleaned from it. The claim that the image on the Shroud is that of Jesus remains controversial, but it is clearly possible, perhaps even more probable than not. I consider the case made by researchers to be strong, and personally accept it. I also acknowledge that I could be mistaken.

Ian Wilson has made a compelling case for the view that the Shroud was kept in the Byzantine Empire for many centuries, where it was considered by the church to be the image of Jesus, from which the icons of the Eastern Church derive. This explains why the traditional view of the face of Jesus resembles the one on the Shroud— perhaps the traditional likeness originally came from the Shroud. Rex Morgan, a Shroud researcher, has even argued that an image on plaster in the Domatilla catacomb in Rome, which resembles the Shroud image, is a painting of Jesus produced in the first century.[21] If Morgan is correct, a painted image of Jesus has survived, produced by someone who knew how he looked (see Plate 8.3).

PLATE 8.3. Image from the Oomatilla catacomb, Rome.

Warner Sallman

Perhaps the most famous recent painting purporting to show us how Jesus appeared is a painting done by Warner Sallman early in the twentieth century. Sallman was born in Chicago in 1892.[22] At an early age he showed a talent for drawing and painting and was fascinated by all kinds of religious art, such as stained glass windows and paintings of biblical scenes. His keen interest in art continued as he grew older. Upon graduation from school, Sallman apprenticed in local art studios while attending night classes at Chicago Art Institute. He was later affiliated with various studios until he established one of his own.

The idea of how he should draw the face of Jesus came to him on a January night in 1924 as he was struggling to produce a cover illustration for a denominational magazine of which he was chief illustrator.

Sallman is said to have seen this likeness in a dream or vision, after much frustration in trying to paint the likeness of Jesus (see Plate 8.4) He described it this way: "In the early hours of the morning before dawn there emerged, in one illuminous moment, a visual picturization of Jesus, so clear and definite. And it appeared to me that I was seated at the drawing board with the completed drawing before me."[23] Sallman's painting resembles the Shroud image.

The picture did not gain much recognition until 1933. Then, when a need was expressed in 1940 for a color edition, Sallman painted it in oils, which then became the basis for many prints. More than six million copies of this painting were distributed during World War II alone, and it is still widely reproduced. According to one estimate, more than 500 million copies have been made.

PLATE 8.4. Warner Sallman's painting of Christ, 1924.

Herbert Beecroft

Beecroft was well-known in his lifetime as an illustrator and carica-turist and as a portrait, landscape, and religious painter.

He was born in Reading, England, in 1864,[24] the son of Joseph John Beecroft, a printer. Herbert continued the business his father had begun, but he also possessed an extraordinary artistic talent. Herbert specialized in portraits and caricatures, and for some years gave "sketching lectures and entertainments" in London and else-where, during which members of the audience were invited onto the stage to have their portraits sketched. This was in addition to more conventional portrait painting in a studio or in people's homes.

In January 1905, at the age of 41, Herbert and his wife Dulcie immigrated to Australia, settling in Wollahra, near Sydney, New

PLATE 8.5. Beecroft's painting of Christ.

South Wales. He soon established himself as a versatile artist, producing postcards of views and portraits. *The Sydney Morning Herald* reported on his Australian debut on April 15, 1905, as follows: "Mr. Herbert Beecroft, lightning sketch lecturer and caricaturist, made his first Australian appearance at the Centenary Hall on Wednesday evening last. During the evening Mr. Beecroft drew sketches of a dozen typical Londoners, and concluded the entertainment with a caricature of a member of the audience."[25] Between 1905 and 1920 he painted portraits of Aborigines at La Perouse, New South Wales, and from 1927 he painted a series of portraits of Jesus Christ, prints of which attracted worldwide sales.[26] He was active in St. Columbia Presbyterian Church in Woolahra, and died in 1951.

Beecroft's most famous painting is that of Jesus Christ, which he titled "The Lord turned and looked upon Peter . . . and Peter remembered" (see Plate 8.5).[27] He is said to have long wished to paint a picture of Christ, and one day, at prayer, "he saw the Saviour in vision. This lasted only a few seconds, but it was long enough to impress itself indelibly on his memory. He rushed out to his wife, exclaiming, 'I have seen the Lord.'"[28] Cliffe writes: "This [painting] he set down in oils, and it was subsequently copied many times. I can remember a copy of it hanging of the wall of my Sunday school superintendent, and finding it distinctly unnerving."[29] The painting that is represented here in this book comes from The Museum of Methodism in London, England, and portrays the background to Christ in darker tones than the reddish tones published in *The Link*. Copies of his painting are for sale from various websites, and I surmise that the differences derive from various copies that Beecroft himself made of the painting. I have only seen the copy on display in The Museum of Methodism. His portrayal of Jesus with ruddy complexion, a short beard, bright blue eyes, and reddish hair, is rather different than traditional views of how he appeared, although the shape of the face and his long hair conform to tradition.

An interesting feature of both Sallman's and Beecroft's work is that the marks associated with the crucifixion, such as bruises or cuts on the head or signs of the crown of thorns, do not appear. This fact might be interpreted to mean that painters bring some of their own expectations of how someone might look in visionary form to their work. On the other hand, these painters' images could also be seen as corroborating the suggestion, which I discussed in Chapter 1, that the post-resurrection form in which Jesus appeared might have varied.

The "Image in Roses"

In 1953 the American Psychological Association published a black-and-white picture in its journal that portrayed a man bearing a similarity to the traditional appearance of Jesus (see Plate 8.6). This picture was published along with some notes about ambiguous images that allow them to be seen in various ways. A well-known illustration of this principle is found in the image of what appears as a duck, which also can be seen as a rabbit. Several other images have been produced that have a similar effect. The point about these is that viewers bring certain expectations to seeing, so that different things might be seen in what is one image. The author of the journal article explained he did not know the source of this apparent depiction of Jesus.

In 1995 I gave a talk on visions of Jesus, and after my presentation a man came up and spoke with me about his understanding of the source of the image in question.[30] Paul Tinsley explained that when he was young he had been given a similar photograph (see Plate 8.7) by his parents, who had acquired it in 1949 from the wife of Rev. David Nelson, who pastored a church in Fauquir, British Columbia.

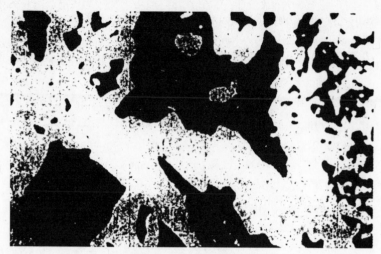

PLATE 8.6. APA illustration, 1953.

PLATE 8.7. Moss's rose photo, circa 1948.

Edith Nelson (nee Moss) had been given it by her mother, who had taken it in about 1948. In Mrs. Moss's front yard was a pretty rose-bush in bloom, and in the spring of that year they had a late snowfall.

The roses looked beautiful nearly covered with snow, so Mrs. Moss decided to take a picture of them. She was surprised to discover that the image that was produced was of figure that resembles Jesus, as he is traditionally viewed. She showed the picture to quite a few people, including her daughter in Fauquir. The Tinsleys were given a copy.

Small differences can be seen between the images in Plates 8.6 and 8.7, although striking similarities also exist. The chin of the Christ-figure in Plate 8.7 is more illuminated than that of the figure in Plate 8.6, for example. The face in Plate 8.7 is more elongated than that of the one in Plate 8.6 as well. Also, more dark background markings are present to the left and the right of the Christ-figure in Plate 8.7. I cannot account for these differences. At some points, Plate 8.6 has more black markings and at other places it has fewer, which suggest that one of these was not formed by simply adding some black markings to a photograph and then generating a different photograph.

To add to the mystery, another version of the image was published as a tract by a Osterhus Publishing House in Minneapolis.[31] It tells the following story:

> In the fall of 1938 an elderly Christian woman of Oslo, Norway, had lost her fellowship with her Lord. She could not pray as she used to, the heavens were like brass to her. She became alarmed about her back-slidden condition. She cried daily to God to give her some assurance—"some definite sign that I am your child. Lord, give me back the joy I had before I left Thee, so I can tell others of Thee and glorify Thy name. Oh! God be merciful to me." This was her continual cry to God.
>
> One day as she was praying to God the still small voice of the Holy Spirit spoke to her plainly, saying: "Take your

camera and go out into the garden and take a picture." She was astonished at the voice and its command, and tried to dismiss it all from her mind; but, the voice spoke again to her with the same words and as plainly as before. This time she was obedient to the voice. She took her camera and went out and snapped the camera at random in the garden. Then she had the film developed, but did not see anything of interest on it, but on a second look, you can well imagine her amazement when she saw the figure of Jesus burst into view!

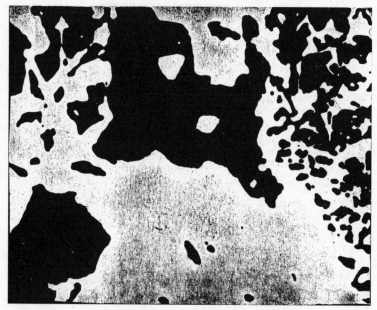

PLATE 8.8. Image published by Osterhus.

The image published is presented here as Plate 8.8, and below it someone from the publishing house has written: "There have been pictures published similar to this one, but with another story. Every one we have seen can be recognized as not original. We bear witness that this picture and story are true." It is of interest to observe that this image differs in details from those in Plates 8.6 and 8.7. I cannot account for these differences.

To add further to the mystery, a letter about the image in question was published in *The Vancouver Sun* on March 23, 1982, written by Kenneth Petter, of Mill Bank, Shalbourne, Wiltshire, in Britain. He writes:

> I first came across it about 1966, when it was sent out on a card by the principal of the Anglican Theological College in Vancouver, the late Rev. John Blewett. With it he sent this story: "The story that is told about this picture is of a Chinese photographer, deeply troubled religiously, who took a picture of the melting snow with black earth showing through. When he developed it he was amazed to see in it the face of Christ full of tenderness and love, and he became a Christian."

Mr. Petter goes on to say that he had made extensive inquiries about who had created the picture, and then requests further information. He evidently had not been satisfied with the explanation offered by Rev. Blewett.

I am inclined to view much of what has been said about this mysterious image of Christ as lacking sufficient documentation, apart from what Mr. Tinsley has supplied. Reports of extraordinary events and experiences need to be well-documented, which includes providing information about the people who were involved and as much detail as possible about the circumstances in which the events or experiences took place.

Concluding Remarks

I consider the Shroud of Turin to be the authentic burial cloth of Jesus, which is a position I came to after about fifteen years of study. I recognize that many of my readers might not be able to concur with me over this controversial matter. However, believing what I do about the Shroud means also that I consider the traditional likeness to be substantially correct. Moreover, because the paintings of both Sallman and Beecroft show strong similarities to the image of the face of the man on the Turin Shroud, I believe they too have pretty much captured the traditional likeness.

Having endorsed the traditional likeness, however, does not mean that I consider the "authenticity" of a vision as dependent upon exhibiting this likeness. I see the issue of authenticity as involving much more than physical appearance, but will not get into that complex issue here. In my view, the question of how Jesus appeared in real life has been substantially answered.

Notes

[1] Ian Wilson, *The Blood and the Shroud* (London: Weidenfeld and Nicolson, 1998), 21.

[2] Ian Wilson, *The Mysterious Shroud* (New York: Doubleday, 1988), 113. Wilson quotes chemistry professor Alan Adler in this section.

[3] Frank C. Tribbe, *Portrait of Jesus?* (New York: Stein and Day, 1983), 175.

[4] Raymond N. Rogers, *A Chemist's Perspective on the Shroud of Turin* (Barrie M. Schwortz: 2008), 15. Rogers was among the group of forty specialists permitted to examine the Shroud for several days in 1978.

[5] Tribbe, *Portrait,* 134.

[6] John P. Jackson, "An Unconventional Hypothesis to Explain all Image Characteristics Found on the Shroud Image," in *Symposium Proceedings: History, Science, Theology and the Shroud,* St. Louis, Missouri, June 22–23, 1991, ed. Aram Berard (Amarillo, Texas: privately published, 1991), 328.

[7] Ian Wilson and Barrie Schwortz, *The Turin Shroud: The Illustrated Evidence* (Toronto: McArthur, 2000), 76.

[8] Thomas Humber, *The Sacred Shroud* (New York: Pocket Books, 1977), 62.

[9] Ibid., 42.

[10] Antonio Gaspari, "The Shadow of a Coin," *Inside the Vatican* (October 1996): 20. See the discussion of the possibility of coins by Antonio Lombatti, "Doubts Concerning the Coins Over the Eyes," *British Society for the Turin Shroud Newsletter* 45 (1997): 35–37.

[11] Tribbe, *Portrait of Jesus?* 163.

[12] Wilson, *The Mysterious Shroud,* 153.

[13] Avinoam Danin, "The Origin of the Shroud of Turin from the Near East as Evidenced by Plant images and Pollen Grains," *Shroud of Turin* website, accessed December 18, 2013, http://www.shroud.com/danin2.htm.

[14] Wilson, *The Blood and the Shroud,* 104f.

[15] This point has been recently disputed, but many Shroud experts do not think that a faint image of the face appears on the "backside" of the cloth.

[16] Mary and Alan Whanger, *The Shroud of Turin: An Adventure in Discovery* (Franklin, Tenn.: Providence House, 1998), chap. 10.

[17] Jackson, "An Unconventional Hypothesis," 328.

[18] Thaddeus Trenn, "The Shroud of Turin: Resetting the Carbon-14 Clock," in *Facets of Faith and Science. Volume 3: The Role of Beliefs in the Natural Sciences,* ed. Jitse M. van der Meer (Lanham, Md.: University Press of America, 1996), 119–33.

[19] See the extensive discussion of the theories of Jackson, Trenn, and also Jean-Baptiste Rinaudo about radiation being the cause of the Shroud image in

Mark Antonacci, *The Resurrection of the Shroud* (New York: M. Evans, 2000), chap. 10.

[20] Brian Walsh, "The 1988 Shroud of Turin Radiocarbon Tests Considered," Paper presented at the Shroud of Turin International Research Conference, Richmond, Virginia, June 18–20, 1999. http://archive.is/gbKJt (accessed January 30, 2014).

[21] Rex Morgan, "The Greatest Secret of the Catacombs? The Search Continues," Paper presented at the Shroud of Turin International Research Conference, Richmond, Virginia, June 18–20, 1999.

[22] "Warner Sallman Biography," on *Christ-Centered Art* website, accessed December 18, 2013, http://www.christcenteredmall.com/stores/art/sallman/sallmanbiography.htm.

[23] Huyssen and Huyssen, *I Saw the Lord*, 137.

[24] See *The Reading Chronicle* (from the UK) for an article by David Cliffe on Beecroft. http://www.readingchronicle.co.uk/articles/1/3660/sdfsdfsfd (accessed on February 11, 2014). Cliffe contributes similar information on a website identified as *Beecroft/Beacroft/Becroft/Becraft/Beacraft/Beecraft's Worldwide: Lawrence Herbert Beecroft,* http://becraft.info/becraft/i5665.htm (accessed January 31, 2014), where his source is identified as *Online Australian Birth-Marriage-Death Index*. Much of this information is corroborated in the New South Wales State Library, "Manuscripts, Oral History, and Pictures," http://acms.sl.nsw.gov.au/item/itemDetailPaged.aspx?itemID=152434 (accessed February 11, 2014).

[25] See http://becraft.info/becraft/i5665.htm.

[26] New South Wales State Library, "Manuscripts, Oral History, and Pictures."

[27] *The Link*, vol. 1 (no. 5), December 1981, 101. This magazine was published by the Christian Israel Foundation, West Midlands, UK.

[28] Ibid.

[29] David Cliffe, *The Reading Chronicle*.

[30] Paul Tinsley, personal communication, followed by a letter dated April 17, 1995, from which the details here were obtained.

[31] The source for this tract and the next letter is Dr. John Anonby, Professor of English for many years at Trinity Western University in Langley, British Columbia.

CHAPTER 9

CONCLUSION

The accounts of visions and appearances of Jesus Christ evidently form a significant part of religious experience. Although the best-known accounts come from people who have lived extraordinary lives of faith and devotion, such as Saint Paul and Saint Teresa of Avila, these experiences have not been restricted to the renowned. Ordinary people, whose lives are not particularly noteworthy in terms of either public or religious service, have also reported experiences that appear to rank in significance with those of people who are justly famous.

I believe it would be a mistake to accept the authenticity only of the experiences of those who have lived publicly exemplary lives and to be suspicious of visions reported by people otherwise unknown. To do so would be establishing prejudgment about the nature of visionary experiences. We cannot know in advance of serious inquiry exactly who might have a vision of Jesus. When we look at the New Testament accounts themselves, we can see that a variety of people had such an encounter.

The closest disciples of Jesus, who were the first to see him after the resurrection, are often seen as examples of goodness. However, Saul the Pharisee, before he became the apostle Paul, had a reputation for persecuting believers even to the point of participating in their deaths when he experienced his first vision of Jesus. The subsequent history of visions of Jesus suggests many of the people who have this experience were neither extremely devout nor extremely wicked, but included a mix of both vice and virtue. Visions of Jesus have been reported frequently enough to be given a place in serious thought about the nature of the world.

Evidence that arises from careful attention to experience does not have the high status of experimental evidence. This fact presents a challenge to experience that is difficult to overcome. Until the rise of modern science, only limited insights into nature at large were available, for experimental work was not done on any significant scale, and the insights that were available were largely obtained through experience. Such limited bodies of knowledge allowed various civilizations to exist, even to flourish occasionally, but experimental knowledge—as opposed to *experiential* knowledge—has allowed science to blossom.

The influential research programs associated with Isaac Newton, Charles Darwin, Albert Einstein, and many others, indicate that an age of experience has been largely replaced by an age of experimentation. Virtually everything once advanced as knowledge on the basis of shared experience has come under critical scrutiny as experimental work has revealed that much of what was once believed is flawed, mistaken, or even incorrectly conceived. Unfortunately, religious beliefs come from the age of experience, and whether such beliefs, mostly derived from the ancient and medieval worlds, have any significant place in modern thought is very much contested.

The fact that visions cannot be obtained at will but occur under circumstances that can hardly be controlled, if at all, means they are not subject to normal scientific testing. The belief that these experiences might not be that significant arises in part because the prevalence of science has brought with it a decline in emphasis upon the data of experience, compared to the data of experiment. I believe it is a mistake to ignore the experiential dimension of human life, particularly when the experiences people report occur often enough to be deserve close attention. I suggest that visions of Jesus belong in this group. They obviously are not part of experimental data, that is, data that can be obtained at will, and therefore dependent only upon the time and resources given to researching them. However, neither do visions of Jesus belong to a group of experiences so seldom reported that we might safely question whether they should be considered in theorizing about the world. The latter data, sometimes described as anecdotal, can perhaps be illustrated by reports of the Loch Ness monster, although doing so runs the risk of raising some controversy.

Visions of Jesus belong to a kind of evidence that is neither anecdotal nor experimental. Such experiences are not so rare that we might responsibly ignore them, but neither are they subject to experimental control so that they fit comfortably into our view of science. I believe greater efforts need to be made to rescue religious experience from being dismissed prematurely by Western culture.

The most important visions for defending the existence of a "spiritual world," or a "spiritual reality," are those in which some change is made to the ordinary world, or those that are seen collectively, that is, by more than one person at once. Although a significant percentage of visions of Jesus are reported to have one or both of these characteristics, most are private experiences whose effect is felt primarily by the person who has the experience. Whether visions of Jesus of one or both of these kinds are numerous enough to form a "critical mass" is uncertain.

I believe another type of experience important in establishing the possibility of a "different kind of reality" occurs when the person experiencing the vision attempts to perform a "reality check," either by turning away and then turning back to look at the point where the vision first appeared, or by attempting to touch the figure that appears in the vision. I spoke earlier about the vision experiences of Helen Bezanson, who looked away and then looked back again to the point where she first saw the figure she identified as Jesus in both of her experiences. I doubt that her experiences were hallucinatory, primarily because of her ability to perform a reality check.

The value of having very detailed information about the nature of a vision experience is clear from this example. I find most of the accounts that have come to us from history to be lacking in such detail. I suppose this lack of detail is understandable because these accounts were perhaps written down by and for people who were not skeptical of a spiritual reality. However, we live in a much more skeptical age, in which detailed information is needed to test various attempts to explain visions.

At this point, other forms of evidence need to be considered to help substantiate that visions might give us some insight into another kind of reality. Other kinds of religious experience suggest this larger "world," so to speak. William James pointed a way forward in a study of religious experience a century ago published as *The Varieties of Religious Experience.* However, relatively little close study of such experiences has been undertaken, compared to the advances in most other sciences. Sir Alister Hardy, a prominent British biologist who was knighted for his work in biology, turned his attention to religious experience toward the end of his career. He opened and funded a modest center for the study of religious experience at Oxford. It has now moved to Wales, and has attempted to take Hardy's work forward. When I visited it in the year 2000, they had approximately 8,000 experiences on file. These generally support the claim that many people are having experiences that suggest the existence of "another reality."

The recent research of Emma Heathcote-James at the University of Birmingham into contemporary reports of encounters with angels is another hopeful indicator that religious experience might be attracting more attention.[1] The 800 reports she collected come from people of all backgrounds: doctors, barristers, teachers, nurses, members of the clergy, homemakers, the unemployed, and prisoners. Moreover, the experiences are not limited to Christians but occur to people who are atheistic, agnostic, or belong to other faiths, including Jewish, Hindu, and Muslim. Some cases involve collective experiences, suggesting that what has been observed is real.

I believe we need to be cautious in asserting that the "spiritual world," if it does exist, is exactly the way it appears to us. Of all people in the history of the world, those who have lived through the great revolution in physics in the twentieth century should understand that things are not exactly as they might appear. The solid brass doorknob is composed of molecules too small to be individually seen, and the atoms that make up the molecules consist of neutrons and protons closely compressed together to form nuclei around which electrons revolve. Moreover, the distance across any given nucleus is miniscule compared to the distance from the nucleus to the electrons revolving around it.

Atomic physics has taught us that reality is rather different than it appears to human beings, whose powers of sight appear to be designed for viewing the "middle sized objects" of the world, rather than those that are very large or very small. I believe we need to bring the humility that science teaches us to our views on the "spiritual world," and see the beings whose existence it asserts as real without presuming to say exactly what that "world" is like. *That* it exists has been given us to know; *how* it exists has not.

Although all visions no doubt carry enough similarities that they can be brought together as one kind of experience, those of Jesus carry special significance, primarily because he is so extraordinary. His resurrection demonstrates that he is God Incarnate, and the appearances and visions in which he is encountered help to make this extraordinary claim credible. This is the significance, as I see it, of these remarkable encounters.

Note

[1] Emma Heathcote-James, *Seeing Angels* (London: John Blake, 2002).

BIBLIOGRAPHY

Anastasias the Librarian. *The Life of St Peter of Alexandria*. The Saint
Pachomius Orthodox Library. http://www.fordham.edu/halsall/basis/
peteralex.asp (accessed March 3, 2014).

Antonacci, Mark. *The Resurrection of the Shroud*. New York: M. Evans,
2000.

Augustine. *The Literal Meaning of Genesis*. Trans. J. H. Taylor. New York:
Newman, 1982.

Baker, H. A. *Visions Beyond the Veil*. Monroeville, Penn.: Whitaker, 1973.

Barnstone, Willis, ed. *The Other Bible*. San Francisco: Harper, 1984.

Baxter, Betty. *The Betty Baxter Story: A 1941 Miracle as Told by Herself*.
Ed. Reverend Don Heidt. Garden City, NY: Country Life Press, 1951.

Brewer, E. Cobham. *A Dictionary of Miracles*. London: Chatto &
Windus, 1884.

Bulgakov, Sergius. *The Orthodox Church*. Crestwood, N.Y.: St. Vladimir's
Seminary, 1988.

Cavendish, Richard. "Ghosts." In *Man, Myth and Magic: An Illustrated
Encyclopedia of the Supernatural*. Ed. Richard Cavendish. New York:
Marshall Cavendish, 1970.

Connell, Janice. *The Visions of the Children: The Apparitions of the
Blessed Mother at Medjugorje*. New York: St. Martin's, 1992.

Davey, Cyril J. *The Story of Sadhu Sundar Singh: The Saint of India.* Bromley, UK: STL Books, 1980.

Deaconus, Marcus. *The Life of Saint Porphyry: Bishop of Gaza.* Trans. G. F. Hill. Oxford: Clarendon Press, 1913.

Emmerich, Anne Catherine. *The Dolorus Passion of Our Lord Jesus Christ.* Rockford, Ill.: Tan Books, 1983.

Esther, Gulshan. *The Torn Veil: The Story of Sister Gulshan Esther.* London: Marshall Pickering, 1992.

Feaver, Karen M. "Chinese Lessons: What Chinese Christians Taught a U.S. Congressional Delegation." *Christianity Today* (May 16, 1994): 33–34.

Gaspari, Antonio. "The Shadow of a Coin." *Inside the Vatican* (October 1996): 20.

Gregory the Great. *Dialogues.* Trans. O. J. Zimmerman. New York: Fathers of the Church, 1959.

Harrison, Ted. *Stigmata: A Medieval Mystery in a Modern Age.* New York: St. Martin's Press, 1994.

Heathcote-James, Emma. *Seeing Angels.* London: John Blake, 2002.

Herbermann, Charles, et. al., eds. *Catholic Encyclopedia.* New York: Robert Appleton, 1912.

Hollands, Ernie. *Hooked.* Toronto: Mainroads, 1983.

Humber, Thomas. *The Sacred Shroud.* New York: Pocket Books, 1977.

Huyssen, Chester, and Lucille Huyssen. *I Saw the Lord.* Tarrytown, N.Y.: Fleming H. Revell, 1992.

———. *Visions of Jesus.* Plainfield, N.J.: Logos International, 1977.

Jackson, John P. "An Unconventional Hypothesis to Explain all Image Characteristics Found on the Shroud Image." *Symposium Proceedings: History, Science, Theology and the Shroud, St. Louis, Missouri, June 22–23, 1991.* Ed. Aram Berard. Amarillo, Texas: Private Publisher, 1991, 325–344.

Julian of Norwich. *The Revelations of Divine Love.* Trans. J. Walsh. London: Burns & Oates, 1961.

Logie, Kenneth. *Stepping Stones to Glory.* New York: Vantage Press, 2001.

Lombatti, Antonio. "Doubts Concerning the Coins over the Eyes." *British Society for the Turin Shroud Newsletter* 45 (1997): 35–37.

Mackenzie, Andrew. *Apparitions and Ghosts: A Modern Study.* London: Arthur Barker, 1971.

Morgan, Rex. "The Greatest Secret of the Catacombs? The Search Continues." Paper presented at the Shroud of Turin International Research Conference. Richmond, Virginia. June 18–20, 1999.

Nixon, Laurence. "Maladjustment and self-actualization in the life of Teresa of Avila." *Studies in Religion/ Sciences Religieuses* 18 (1989): 283–95.

Roberts, A., and J. Donaldson, eds. "The Book of John Concerning the Falling Asleep of Mary." *The Writing of the Fathers Down to A.D. 325.* Grand Rapids, Mich.: Eerdmans, 1956.

Rogers, Raymond N. *A Chemist's Perspective on the Shroud of Turin.* Florissant, CO: Barrie M. Schwortz, 2008.

Schaff, Philip, ed. *Nicene and Post-Nicene Fathers of the Christian Church, Second Series.* Edinburgh: T & T Clark: 1886–1900.

Schneemelcher, Wilhelm. *New Testament Apocrypha,* vol. 1, rev. ed. Cambridge: James Clarke & Co., 1991.

Schouppe, F. X. *Purgatory: Illustrated in the Lives and Legends of the Saints.* London: Burns, Oates and Washbourne, 1920.

Sigstedt, Cyriel Odhner. *The Swedenborg Epic: The Life and Works of Emanuel Swedenborg.* New York: Bookman, 1952.

Sparrow, Scott. *I am With You Always: True Stories of Encounters with Jesus.* New York: Bantam Books, 1995.

Swedenborg, Emanuel. *Spiritual Diary of Emanuel Swedenborg: Being the Record during Twenty Years of His Supernatural Experience.* Trans. George Bush and John H. Smithson. London: Swedenborg Foundation, 1971.

Tafel, Rudolph L. *Documents Concerning Swedenborg. Volume 1: The Life and Character of Emanuel Swedenborg.* London: Swedenborg Society, 1875.

Teresa of Avila. *The Life of the Holy Mother Teresa of Jesus.* Trans. E. Allison Peers. London: Sheed & Ward, 1946.

Trenn, Thaddeus. "The Shroud of Turin: Resetting the Carbon-14 Clock." *Facets of Faith and Science. Volume 3: The Role of Beliefs in the Natural Sciences.* Ed. Jitse M. van der Meer. Lanham, Md: University Press of America, 1996.

Tribbe, Frank C. *Portrait of Jesus?* New York: Stein and Day, 1983.

Tyrrell, G. N. M. *Apparitions.* London: Gerald Duckworth, 1942.

Walsh, Brian. "The 1988 Shroud of Turin Radiocarbon Tests Considered." Paper presented at the Shroud of Turin International Research Conference, Richmond, Virginia, June 18–20, 1999. http://archive.is/gbKJt (accessed January 30, 2014).

Walsh, William J. *The Apparitions and Shrines of Heaven's Bright Queen.* New York: Cary-Stafford, 1906.

Wesley, John. *The Works of John Wesley. Volume 22: Journal and Diaries V (1765–75).* Eds. W. Reginald Ward and Richard P. Heitzenrater. Nashville, TN: Abingdon Press, 1993.

West, Louis J. "A Clinical and Theoretical Overview of Hallucinatory Phenomena." In *Hallucinations: Behavior, Experience and Theory.* Eds. R.K. Siegel and L.J. West. New York: Wiley, 1975. 287–311.

Whanger, Mary, and Alan Whanger. *The Shroud of Turin: An Adventure in Discovery.* Franklin, Tenn.: Providence House, 1998.

White, John. *Putting the Soul Back in Psychology.* Downers Grove, Ill.: Intervarsity, 1987.

Wiebe, Phillip H. "The Christic Visions of Teresa of Avila." *Scottish Journal of Religion* 20 (1999): 73–87.

———. "Critical Reflections on Christic Visions." In *Cognitive Models and Spiritual Maps.* Eds. Jensine Andresen and Robert K. C. Forman. Special issue, *The Journal of Consciousness Studies, Controversies in Science and the Humanities* 7 (2000): 119–44.

———. *Visions of Jesus: Direct Encounters from the New Testament to Today.* New York: Oxford University Press, 1997.

Wilson, Ian. *The Blood and the Shroud.* London: Weidenfeld and Nicolson, 1998.

———. *The Mysterious Shroud.* New York: Doubleday, 1988.

Wilson Ian, and Barrie Schwortz. *The Turin Shroud: The Illustrated Evidence.* Toronto: McArthur, 2000.